LEADERSHIP LAUNCH

ESSENTIAL SKILLS FOR NEW LEADERS

LEADERSHIP LAUNCH

ESSENTIAL SKILLS FOR NEW LEADERS

DERRICK NOBLE

MALCOLM&BALDWIN
PUBLISHING

2022

Lionel Ward

This book is dedicated to the memory
of the man I most admired.

My very first mentor;

My very first personal example of great leadership;

My principal from 5th-6th grade at Rightsell
Intermediate School, Little Rock, Arkansas;

Mr. Lionel Ward: 1954-2021

CONTENTS

I am Dr. Melba Pattillo-Beals, one of the nine teenagers who integrated Central High School in 1957, amidst the historic states' rights firestorm. It was an event that necessitated the nine of us being guarded by the 101st Airborne Division to shield us from rampaging mobs who were determined to define our equality by restrictions derived from the past.

Thirty years later, we were blessed to have accomplished our goal and survived, having previously risked our lives to complete school terms that resulted in the KKK posting $10,000 dead and $5,000 alive on our heads during the spring of 1958. As teenagers, we were compelled to escape Little Rock, thus abandoning our families and dismantling our community foundations to save our lives. Accordingly, we would begin our young adult lives in safe havens such as California, Canada, and Norway.

In 1987, all nine of us—then as healthy, thriving adults—were invited to return to Central High School for five days of pomp and circumstance, enfolded in loving care and even some gratitude from local community members, some of whom in 1957 wanted to be rid of us by any means possible. Returning to the scene of our incredible experience together for the first time, we had come to give thanks and celebrate the contributions that we had made towards toppling traditional walls of segregation. It was my privilege to be a part of the 30-year anniversary.

To celebrate the occasion, the initial part of our program began at Central High School. One of the first young people to greet us was Derrick Noble. He was an African American young man who would soon become an individual who I would never forget. As the president of the 2,000-member student body, which had become a tapestry of races, I could only imagine the work it took to be voted into office amidst lingering Southern attitudes of racism.

Wearing a morning coat, he looked at each of us in the eye and bowed with a genuine smile of welcome. Thereafter, he became our escort, directing us up the stairs and into the front door. He was a welcome guide, especially for those of us who were very apprehensive about returning to this scene that had caused us so much heartache and pain. With his words, manner, and expression, he commanded our full attention. It was immediately apparent that he had prepared for our visit. Notably, he made me feel special and calmed my nerves so that I could focus on an occasion that I had waited a lifetime to experience.

During those moments, some of the members of the welcoming team referred to us as the Mississippi Twelve or Tennessee Five instead of the Little Rock Nine. By that time, having already traveled across the country, I had accepted the fact that not everyone knew who we were. Nevertheless, here at Central High School, I had assumed that all the students would be prepared to greet us with knowledge of this historic act that had taken place at their high school.

Indeed, Mr. Noble demonstrated his serious pursuit of knowledge and willingness to go beyond what was required by somehow securing the morning coat and knowledge of what courtesy meant to us. Moreover, his ability and willingness to behave in a certain manner, although quite unlike some of his fellow classmates, demonstrated his leadership. In the face of all who surrounded him, his behavior certainly accorded us his highest order of respect.

Throughout the day, I yearned to talk to him. In fact, I took every opportunity to ask questions about what he wanted to be when he grew up, what he was studying, and how he was elected president of student body. With each answer, I became more convinced that this young man could one day become president of the United States if he desired. I was most impressed by his respect for fellow human beings. His willingness to share and acknowledgement of others demonstrated his maturity

After that ceremony, when several of us nine gathered, we each referred to Derrick Noble as a young man who was destined to be successful—a young man with a sympathetic and sincere determination. We all shared the same feeling that Derrick was destined for success. Most of all, it was clear that this young man would contribute to the community, as he clearly understood his obligation to function at his best.

I would remember Derrick throughout my life, and when I wrote my book, **Warriors Don't Cry**, I specifically mentioned how impressed I was with him. I had followed him as an adult, noting his work as he developed into a renowned business coach and speaker. Everything that we predicted and more has come true.

I believe that Derrick Noble is a most special human being who inspires others to give their personal best, most notably because he always demonstrates what he requires from others. His belief that everyone else is already special and only needs work to demonstrate their incredible talents is key to his ability to coach. His commitment is clear regarding the belief that we all must support each other in our efforts to demonstrate our personal best as we serve each other at the highest level.

I am confident in recommending Derrick Noble's book because it is written as he speaks: with clarity and simplicity. In the process, he shares the inspiring steps that he took to achieve his goals. It is a map to the step-by-step climb associated with practicing effective leadership, and it will benefit those who wish to elevate their ability to lead and enhance team membership by describing the skills required.

Beginners, intermediates, and those at the pinnacle of leadership who are resting on an unstable ladder will find this book to be a wonderful push forward to achieve leadership success. Derrick Noble's book will not only benefit leaders, but also those who follow them.

INTRODUCTION

In my mind, I had made it. It was the mid-90s, I was in my mid-twenties, and I had just received my graduate degree as class valedictorian only two weeks prior. It was my first day on my first full-time job, and while the pay wasn't great, the job came with a title: I was a departmental director. It was a brand-new department, so I was its first leader—ever. The CEO had heard me give a presentation a few months earlier at a national leadership gathering in Chicago and was so impressed that he hired me on the spot to head this new department he was developing. I hadn't even officially graduated yet when I had delivered that two-hour presentation on mobilizing volunteers for non-profit organizations, and I suddenly had a job waiting for me—as a department head! Everything was falling into place.

I had my own office in a brand new, multi-million-dollar building. The mahogany furniture was accented with a plush, burgundy, leather executive's chair that was as soft as pudding. The wall was replete with abstract artwork, and the office administrator had a surprise for me: my degrees were already hanging on the wall, each in the fanciest golden picture frames I had ever seen. I had my own private computer already loaded with this new thing called the WorldWideWeb. I had heard it was the perfect resource for conducting research, which would be a major requirement of this new position.

I even had an assistant director; a really nice guy a couple years younger than me, who also was a first-time leader. We had met a week earlier as I was moving into my new rental home, and we had hit it off very well. We were both young and super excited to have an opportunity such as this one. This was going to be awesome.

As we both sat in my luxurious office on my very first day, he looked at me and smiled. "Okay, so, um, where do we start? What are we supposed to do first?"

My smile quickly faded, as it dawned on me that I only had one, embarrassing answer to his query: "Wow…I really don't know. I honestly haven't the slightest idea *where* to start."

He chuckled a little and said, "At least I'm not alone in that. But didn't they give you any info during your training sessions?"

"What training sessions? They just told me, 'You're an A student, an excellent communicator, and you come highly recommended. You're going to kill it!'"

We fell silent, and just stared at each other uncomfortably.

Does this sound familiar?

Maybe you, too, have celebrated a big promotion into leadership, but then, once the celebration is over and once the noise has died down, a frightening reality hits: "I know how to be a great employee— that's why they gave me a promotion. But what I *don't* know how to be is a great leader, manager, or supervisor.

That reality is quickly followed by these revelations:

- The actions and skills that got me to this point will not necessarily translate into my being a strong leader.
- I have excelled as an individual, but now I must excel in leading a team of individuals—something I don't have much experience in.
- I have successfully completed my projects early or on time, but now I bear the responsibility of enabling an entire team of people to do the same.
- I successfully moved myself up the corporate ladder, but now I must lead a team to victory within this organization.

Again, reality hits: "What got me here will not be enough to get me where I need to be."

If you can relate – if, indeed, you've lost sleep over your new position as a leader – this book is for you. While I once was climbing the corporate ladder myself, nowadays I invest my time helping new (and even some seasoned) leaders learn how to effectively lead. I teach them how to stay focused on making the right decisions and reduce their stress levels, all while creating shortcuts to being more effective.

Therefore, this book covers those three primary lessons in leadership success:

1. **Focus on the right details**
2. **Reduce stress, and**
3. **Create shortcuts to effectiveness.**

New leaders and seasoned leaders alike can benefit from this information. So long as you are willing to change and want to lead your team to success, this book is for you.

The information in this book comes from various sources: my mentors over the years, my own experiences, my successes, my failings, etc., and is designed to help you skip over that risky period of trial and error as best as possible. Hopefully, by the end of this book, you will be equipped with all the tools I wish I had in that plush, burgundy office.

But before jumping into the nitty gritty, let's discuss why you need to reduce your learning curve at all, and the benefits you can gain from doing so.

Why You Need to Hit the Ground Running

One of the best ways to become an effective leader who permanently and positively impacts the lives of others while also improving the culture of an organization is to create shortcuts to effectiveness, or to reduce what I like to call the "leadership learning curve." That fact is one of the reasons this book is entitled "Leadership Launch." The goal is to help you hit the ground running, or to help launch you forward in your leadership proficiency as quickly as possible. Let's explore this concept a bit further.

"Learning curve" is a phrase first used by German psychologist Hermann Ebbinghaus in 1879. Ebbinghaus theorized that increasing the amount of material to be learned consequently increased the amount of time necessary to learn said material. The length of one's learning curve "plays a key role in determining how fast [one will] be successful when [one] embark[s] on a new enterprise or career."[1] Especially early in my career, much of what I learned about being a successful leader came from lots of trial-and-error learning, which, in hindsight, equated to lots of wasted time – a luxury you can ill-afford. Had I known where my focus *should* have been, I would have been much less frazzled and stressed out, and that would have helped me to become a better, stronger, more proficient leader in a shorter amount of time.

While it may be unfair, it is still a fact: those who hired you are expecting to see results quickly. Although being an emerging leader means that all or most of this is quite new to you, the truth is, you do not have the luxury of being able to take too much time to produce results. Most leaders mistakenly equate "quick" with "sloppy." Don't be one of them.

It is possible to steer the ship (or even right the ship) quickly without losing any of your precious cargo. You were placed into your position because someone, somewhere, had the confidence that you could do it. Everyone involved is invested in your success, and wasting time is a luxury you simply cannot afford. That is why producing results quickly is so important.

---

[1] John Wood, 15 Tips for Reducing Your Learning Curve. American Writers and Artists Institute. April 18, 2012. https://www.awai.com/2012/04/cut-your-learning-curve/

For most leaders, this type of pressure creates great anxiety, fear, and pain. I understand that, but I also understand that it doesn't *have* to create anxiety, fear, and pain. You want those who hired you and the people you now lead to view you as the go-to person, the expert leader they have needed all along. You want the people you lead to admire you and most gladly want to follow you. You want to avoid years of frustrating trial-and-error learning. You want to distinguish yourself from other leaders in your industry. I know that's what you want, because most leaders *don't* want those things—and you're not most leaders. You're not happy with being run-of-the-mill, with just collecting your salary and sticking to the status quo. You want to do well as a leader. That's why you're here.

Within those three primary lessons in leadership success that form the foundation of this book – namely 1) focusing on the right details so that 2) the leader can be less stressed out in order to 3) get the work of leadership accomplished more quickly, thereby creating shortcuts to effectiveness - this book will provide the following five strategies that will also help you hit the ground running in your new leadership position. They are:

1. Learning the abilities and attitudes of each employee you lead.
2. Knowing how to motivate your workforce.
3. Becoming an exceptionally skilled communicator.
4. Having the right support team in your corner; and
5. Mastering the fine art of delegation.

You will learn Strategies 1 and 2 in the very next chapter, while you will learn Strategies 3, 4, and 5 in the last chapter. I have arranged this particular content in this way so that each strategy is discussed within whichever of the three primary lessons in leadership success it happens to fall. For example, Strategies 1 and 2 help you to focus on the right details of leadership, while Strategies 3, 4, and 5 help you to create shortcuts to effectiveness.

That second primary lesson in leadership – effectively managing stress - has its own dedicated chapter, since my years of experience as well as my research for this book have revealed that the topic of stress is the one area with which most new leaders appear to need the greatest amount of help.

The principles you will be learning in this book are not industry specific. They are in fact universal, and that is great news for you as an emerging leader. For more than 20 years now, I have successfully shared this material as a keynote speaker, trainer, and coach, in-person and virtually, to: leaders of not-for-profit organizations and for-profit organizations.

- US government agencies, including the FBI, the IRS, the US Department of Labor, The US Forestry Commission, and the Social Security Administration.
- Branches of the US military, including the US Air Force and the US Navy at Pearl Harbor, Hawaii.
- Professional associations such as the American Bar Association.
- Colleges, universities, and school district leaders; and
- Leaders from all educational backgrounds, genders, races, and cultures in every region of the United States.

These principles are applicable across the board, so regardless of where you find yourself, by reading this book you have already taken the first few steps on your journey to become the leader you have always known you could be.

If you apply what you learn on these pages:

- You will save time with a proven and predictable process to create meaningful outcomes.
- You will avoid years of frustrating trial-and-error learning.
- You will be seen as the "go-to person" within your organization and perhaps even within your industry.

- You will never again feel like you're lost in the crowd.
- You will create even more career opportunities for yourself.
- You will attract more of the clients with whom you want to do business; and
- You will advance faster in your career.

The Three Possible Reactions

Whenever I begin a presentation, I never fail to inform my audience that there are typically **three reactions** a person can have to any type of presentation, whether it's a seminar, a webinar, an in-person class, a keynote presentation, etc.:

Reaction #1: I already knew that. Some of the information you find on these pages will be information you already know and are currently applying. You should celebrate that fact, because that means you already have confidence and knowledge in this area, thus providing a boost of self-esteem and a burst of momentum as you head into future challenges. You've already laid the groundwork, so the later lessons will be easier for you to implement.

For example, I had taken a class in basic Greek when I was a high school student. Six years later, during my first year of graduate school, Greek was one of the requirements for my degree program. I confidently approached a class that had earned a campus-wide reputation for being one of the more difficult courses in the entire graduate program, and I earned an A. The fact that I already knew basic Greek gave me confidence going into that course and helped me to earn the grade that I earned. Admittedly, at first, I was a little bored as we reviewed things I already knew, but the review strengthened my knowledge and made it come more easily to me. Plus, since I already had a foundation, the more difficult grammar and syntax was easier since I wasn't grappling so much with the basics as the rest of the class was.

So, as you read and you come across information that you already know, celebrate the fact that you already bring a wealth of knowledge to your new role as a leader. And, instead of skipping ahead, welcome the opportunity to solidify your strengths even more.

Reaction #2: I knew that, but I had forgotten; thanks for the reminder. There are some things we know or may have heard before, but for whatever reason we are not currently applying them. This, too, is a gift. It is that kick in the pants that we need that tells us, "Okay, you know you should be doing this, so why aren't you?" We all need reminders from time to time. For example, we all know that we should not only brush our teeth but that we should floss regularly. Flossing is one of those things we all know we should do but we don't always do. So, hearing the dentist prompt you of its importance is a reminder that we all occasionally need. A psychologist friend of mine recently told me that the average adult needs to hear something seven times before it sinks in and registers. When you're at the point of being tired of saying it, the person to whom you're saying it is probably just beginning to remember it and practice it.

As you read and come across those reminders of things you know to do but don't always follow through on, celebrate the fact that you now can do whatever is necessary to move yourself closer to making it a regular part of your daily routine.

Reaction #3: I never knew that! This is definitely a cause for celebration. As a leader, if you are not growing daily, then you are declining daily; there is no other option. Get excited about the new information you are about to learn and make a commitment to do something with the new information you receive—immediately share it with someone else; immediately apply it to your own life and leadership situation; circle, highlight, underline it; heck, tattoo it on your bicep if need be! I set a goal for myself years ago to learn at least one new fact, every day of my life. You don't "know it all," and you never will. How exciting, that there will always be more to learn!

I invite you to celebrate each of these reactions that you will undoubtedly have as you read this book. In fact, at the end of each chapter, I will give you a space to record your reactions and to decide upon some action steps going forward.

Especially if you are a new leader, you will have a lot of the third reaction—that of learning something new. You might feel like this is a bad thing, but in fact, it could be your greatest asset.

My Journey - The Power of Not Knowing

You may not believe it, but the greatest advantage you have as an emerging leader is that you are very aware—sometimes *painfully* aware—that there is so much that you do not know. I'll share a secret with you: that is exactly where you *want* to be!

I memorized the following poem when I was a third grader. I have since seen this poem attributed to everyone from Confucius to an ancient Arabian prince to martial arts legend Bruce Lee. While the authorship may be uncertain, the message is abundantly clear. I present it here, with slightly altered language to make it more gender inclusive:

> *"[The one] who knows not, and knows not that [they] know not,*
> *is a fool: shun [them].*
> **[The one] who knows not, and knows that [they] know not, is a**
> **student: teach [them].**
> *[The one] who knows, and knows not that [they] know, is asleep: awaken*
> *[them].*
> *[The one] who knows, and knows that [they] know, is wise: follow [them]."*

That second line of the poem ought to resonate with you. As a new leader, there is so much you do not know. Right now, you could probably fill a book with what you don't know. Does that make you stupid? Dumb? An in-over-your-head, terrible leader? No—it makes you a student, and we all know what a student needs most: a capable, experienced, patient teacher. That is exactly why I wrote this book.

I want to be the mentor to you that my late elementary school principal, Mr. Lionel Ward, was to me.

I was the youngest of eight children born to Willie and Lillie Mae Noble in Little Rock, Arkansas. I was seven years old on May 4, 1978, when my mother died of a heart attack in her sleep. On that morning, while I was attempting to wake her so she could take me to the bus stop, I began to scream. The noise I made awakened my father who was lying next to her, and it awakened the rest of my siblings, who subsequently stormed our parents' bedroom only to have the patriarch of the family announce that "Momma" had passed away during the calm of the night. My family was never the same. Shortly thereafter, my father had to be committed to the Arkansas State Hospital, an institution for the mentally unstable, and at that point some of my older siblings became the legal guardians of their three youngest siblings.

I had already been seeing the school's speech therapist daily because of my severe stutter and lisp. Of course, my speech impediment made me the target of merciless teasing and even bullying at school. I even remember one of my teachers laughing at me in class, when I couldn't get past the "D" in my own name. But on the day I discovered my mother's body, my stutter became markedly worse. My life was a mess: both of my parents were gone; I felt ugly and was often told I was such (due to major burn scars on my nose, neck, and body from a childhood accident at home); and I felt stupid because I couldn't talk. I was the target of both verbal and physical abuse, daily.

And then came the man who would become my very first mentor and model of leadership.

At the start of my 5th grade year at Rightsell Intermediate School in Little Rock, we received a new principal: a tall, 20-something first year school administrator named Lionel Ward. He drove a silver two-seater Corvette and was the best dressed man I had ever seen. His presence and impact were felt immediately. Rightsell, an inner-city school, had been notorious for fighting on the playground and even in the classrooms. Mr. Ward made it very clear from day one that he would have none of that on his watch.

He spoke with passion about creating a safe environment where unbridled learning would be the new order of the day. Mr. Ward's rule was, "If a fight breaks out, I will personally break it up, and the combatants will be immediately suspended—along with any and everybody who has gathered to *watch* the fight." Before long, where kids would once run to playground skirmishes and yell, "Fight, fight, fight," eventually kids would start to run *away* from playground fights. The playground became a safer place, where kids could play without worrying about getting punched all the time.

I finally had a face-to-face meeting with him after having admired him and respected him from a distance all school year. I was in the library during recess time because I didn't fit in with my classmates. My teachers were kind enough to give me a library pass so that I could avoid the awkwardness and name calling that I often experienced outside at recess. As I sat quietly at a table reading *The World Book Encyclopedia*—my favorite book—a shadow suddenly hovered over me. I turned around to see Mr. Ward in a navy blue, double-breasted suit with gold buttons, a red knit tie, and crisp white shirt. I assumed I was in trouble because I was skipping recess.

He bellowed at me, stone-faced, "I don't know you. Why don't I know you?"

I stared at him, about to cry (as was typically the case when anyone spoke to me in an authoritative voice).

He sensed my fear, put his hand on my shoulder, smiled, and said, "Oh, I know why I don't know you. It's because the students I have gotten to know so far are the troublemakers, and you *clearly* are not one. What's your name, son?"

I stuttered "D-d-d-Derrick, sir. Derrick Noble."

"Hmmm, 'Sir' huh? Intelligent, well-behaved, a reader, *and* polite. That's my favorite kind of student."

He then sat down at the table with me and listened as I told him why I was hiding in the library, and about the death of my mother. He asked me about the types of books I enjoyed reading, walked the shelves with me and gave me some books *he* wanted me to read— books about George Washington Carver, Benjamin Banneker, and Harriet Tubman.

He said, as he was filling my little arms with books, "You know, Derrick, the more you read, the better you read. Promise me you will always enjoy reading, okay?"

Toward the end of the next day, Mr. Ward's voice boomed over the intercom in my 5th grade classroom: "Mrs. Kay, please send Derrick Noble to my office immediately. He's going to be reading our afternoon announcements for the entire student body today."

My classmates, many of whom had made fun of my speech impediment, silently stared at me as I walked out of the classroom and made my way down two flights of stairs to Mr. Ward's office. As soon as I walked in, I opened my mouth to speak, intending to tell him that this was going to be a huge mistake, but he immediately cut me off.

"Don't even say it, son. Don't you *dare* tell me you can't read the announcements because you're a stutterer. You are more than your stutter, understand? *You are a reader.* Now, look at this paper, and practice reading these announcements. You're on in five minutes."

I began stuttering and lisping my way through the announcements that day, all the while telling myself, "They're all laughing at me; I know they are." Then I noticed Mr. Ward's shadow looming over me. I paused, looked up, and saw him smile. He gave me the thumbs up – and so I kept reading. My confidence grew with each word I read. When I completed the final sentence, Mr. Ward immediately grabbed the intercom microphone and said, "Boys and girls, teachers, and staff, that was Derrick Noble - one of this school's best readers. Let's all give him a round of applause." And then I heard it: the student body was loudly applauding and even cheering for me from the various classrooms throughout that three-story building. I would never have imagined that the same people who had once ridiculed me would eventually applaud me.

I read the school announcements many more days after that, slowly but surely becoming less self-conscious about my speech impediment. I still stuttered, but I didn't seem to notice it as much as I once had. And during my 6th grade year, I read the announcements *every* day, because that was Mr. Ward's newly assigned duty for the Student Council President! That's right—at Mr. Ward's insistence, just one year after hiding from my classmates during recess, I had run for student council president, and I had won. That was my very first leadership position, and it happened because I—a scared, stuttering 5th grader—had met an educator who would not allow me to remain a scared stutterer. As a result of that meeting in the library, my grades skyrocketed and I became known as a nerd, a bookworm, a great public speaker, and a student leader—and I enjoyed every minute of it. Mr. Ward took me all over the Little Rock School District and even to school board meetings in his two-seater Corvette, proudly introducing me as his Student Council president, his mentee (a word that he taught me), and his most intelligent student.

Mr. Ward believed in me when I didn't believe in myself. Indeed, his belief in me is what eventually led to me believing in myself. As he often told me, "Muhammad Ali called himself 'The Greatest' before he actually was. That is precisely *why* he became The Greatest." My only regret is that Mr. Ward did not live to see this book get published. Fortunately, he did hear me tell him that I would write it someday and dedicate it to him.

I am where I am today because of the great people who led me here. I have seen, firsthand, the power of leaders and mentors. With some guidance, you, too, can make the permanent, positive impact on someone's life that Mr. Ward made on mine.

So why am I writing this book? Why do I travel the world speaking and training? Why do I have as many one-on-one coaching clients as I do? It's all because I want to be to you the type of mentor Lionel Ward was to me. And I want you to be that type of mentor to the people you lead. I am honored and proud to partner with you on your quest for success. I believe you can do this, emerging leader. Don't you *dare* tell me you can't. Now, start reading—you're on in five minutes.

The Emerging Leader

Any discussion of emerging leaders should probably begin with a definition of the term "emerging leader." Being classified as an "emerging leader" has nothing to do with one's age or one's official job title. One can be a 25-year-old vice-president in an air-conditioned office on the 59th floor or a 45-year-old dock supervisor at a manufacturing plant—both can be emerging leaders.

For our purposes, we will begin by defining an emerging leader as *one who is relatively new to one's leadership position, having served no more than one year on the job.* An emerging leader is a first-time leader, one who has not previously served in a leadership position before within their organization.

To take this definition even further, some within the business community and other leadership circles define emerging leaders as leaders who:

- Are in the process of launching (or re-launching) their careers.
- Are driven to make a difference but trying to identify their core purpose.
- Possess the ability to identify pain points and address all sides of the problem.
- Understand how to articulate their ideas and goals.

- Are good team players or good teammates.
- Are not afraid of change or of being change makers.[2]

Deb Calvert, the president of People First Productivity Solutions of Kansas City, Missouri, says that, if you are an emerging leader, you meet at least one of the following 10 requirements:

1. You are a high performer in your organization.
2. You show high potential in your current role.
3. You informally influence others.
4. You supervise others.
5. You are open to learning, failing, and growing.
6. You have strong people-building skills.
7. You are centered by your core values.
8. You see possibilities for a better future state.
9. You unite others and help them see new possibilities.
10. 10. You want to become a leader. [3]

Given these many definitions and interpretations, the earlier point I made should become clear: being an emerging leader is less about age and title and is more about the amount of time in one's position of leadership, as well as one's character, mindset, and attitude. As you might already be sensing, being new is not always a terrible thing.

The Advantages of Being a New Leader

You may think there are not any advantages to your anxiety as a new leader, and wish you could just wave a wand and have all the

---

[2] https://www.linerun.co/what-is-an-emerging-leader
[3] Deb Calvert, 10 Signs You Are (or could be) an Emerging Leader . LinkedIn. March 24, 2015 https://www.linkedin.com/pulse/10-signs-you-could-emerging-leader-deb-calvert/

confidence of a seasoned pro. However, the very source of your anxiety—the fact that you are new and do not know exactly how things should be run—may very well be your greatest secret weapon of success. Being new and inexperienced carries with it some distinct advantages—advantages, I might add, that seasoned leaders may not necessarily have at their disposal. Let's take a closer look.

Newness Works In Your Favor

I'm not sure who originally said it, but the adage is definitely true: the most dangerous seven words uttered by a leader or by an organization are, "we've never done it that way before." As a new leader, you are not necessarily burdened with the baggage of "the way things used to be" or "how it has always been," and this can seriously work to your advantage.

I have often heard well-meaning people tell new leaders to go slowly and not make any changes during their first few weeks on the job. The idea is that one must be a bit more seasoned before implementing anything new. My advice is the exact opposite. You are new, and people are expecting a certain newness from you. This is the *perfect* time to try that ambitious idea the previous leader was reluctant to try.

Of course, you will need to know the workplace and the people you work with to know what kinds of changes would be beneficial to make. Scheduling some one-on-one time with each member of your team is an essential step, and this should be done within the first *week* of your leadership (not the first month or quarter). While it is extremely important that you get to know the people you lead—and understand that change may create anxiety for them—it is still very possible to make tremendous changes early on. In fact, while it may seem like it, you do not—as we discussed in the introduction—have the luxury of moving slowly. Those who hired you are expecting to see some results *sooner* rather than later. And, if they don't see positive changes soon, they may terminate you and try someone else.

The idea that people do not like change is untrue; what people do not like is unexplained or poorly executed change. We will discuss this more in Chapter 4. For now, just understand that change is expected of you, so do not be afraid to implement it. Also keep in mind that if you wait *too* long to do something new, that dreaded characteristic of becoming jaded may cripple your leadership potential.

Emerging Leaders Are Often Less Jaded

Far too many seasoned leaders—those who have served in a leadership capacity for many years—have become jaded. In other words, they have lost that cutting edge, that sense of adventure that propelled them into leadership in the first place. You will often hear them say things like this to emerging leaders: "I was once as naïve and gung-ho as you are now, but then reality set in." They often say this with a smug smile, as if they wear their jadedness as a badge of honor.

Shortly after I became the new leader of another nonprofit organization, I had a conversation with a seasoned leader. I was in my late 20s, and he was in his 60s. He invited me to lunch and asked me about my vision for the organization. He was a leader of a similar organization in the same city, and had been friends with my predecessor, who had just passed away.

As I shared my hopes and dreams for the organization, he just chuckled as he ate his big plate of spaghetti and meatballs. In fact, he didn't even look up at me; he kept his eyes on his plate.

Sensing the sour mood and his attitude, I stopped sharing and bluntly—yet respectfully—asked, "What's the problem?"

His response?

"Boy, just stay there for a while; you'll see. Those people are crazy. The way they treated my friend and even threatened to take him to court—I can't believe he let them push him around like that. I'm convinced that's what killed him; he was much too young to have died. My people are crazy too, but I've been there long enough that I know how to go toe-to-toe with 'em. Come back and see me in a few months—no, make that a few weeks. I'm sure you'll be singing a different tune."

I began to see the purpose of this luncheon invitation: this guy was so angry about how he felt the organization had treated his friend that he wanted very much to discourage me and warn me about the mess of an organization into which I was walking. He wanted to scare me. In short, it was a sabotage.

Well, I'm from Little Rock, Arkansas and my Black, Southern US culture taught me not to disrespect my elders. I quietly got up from the table, smiled, and said, "Thanks for the advice, sir."

Then I went on to lead that organization through four years of unprecedented numerical and financial growth. I even led the organization to begin giving money to help other nonprofit organizations within the community, an act that created plenty of goodwill for us.

My many years as a leader have never been 100 percent smooth and turbulence free, but I can honestly say that my refusal to be like that jaded, 60-something-year-old leader pushed me forward in some great ways, and for that, I am eternally grateful to him. I am now closer to 60 than I am to my 20s, and yet I have not lost my positive mindset.

Your having less time in your position as a leader works to your advantage because that sense of jadedness has not made you its victim. Don't allow it to do so. Here are my top ten suggestions for avoiding that destructive mentality:

1. Constantly remind yourself of the reasons why you became a leader in the first place. I see leadership as an opportunity to help others to grow, and to change their lives for the better. In fact, my leadership mantra is, "Derrick Noble's purpose is to make a permanent, positive impact on the world by modeling effective leadership and teaching those leadership principles to others." I recite that to myself daily—yes, daily. It keeps me focused and prevents my work from becoming stale. Find your own purpose and remind yourself of it often—or, if you find that difficult, have an important person in your life remind you of it regularly. One of my favorite quotes comes from country music recording artist Shania Twain: "A friend is someone who knows the song in your heart and can sing it back to you when you have forgotten the words."[4]

2. Occasionally, do something kind and charitable for absolutely no reason, and expect nothing in return. As my former graduate school professor Carolyn Ann Knight was fond of saying to her students, "Remember: it's just nice to be nice. Kindness is its own reward." I firmly believe that living a life that doesn't make you the center of it has a way of keeping your heart from becoming calloused and hard. Whether it's volunteering at a soup kitchen, anonymously donating funds to a shelter for abused and battered women and children, giving away turkeys to hungry families every Thanksgiving, or buying the meal for the people in the car behind you at the drive-through window, performing random acts of kindness will have an amazing effect upon your attitude about life and work.

3. Never be hard on yourself about your own emotions or feelings. Who among us has never had a difficult day? At the same time, who among us has made ourselves feel guilty for having that difficult day? We have all done that before. The next time you're feeling down, upset, or discouraged, acknowledge it, thank the universe for reminding you of your own humanity, and tell yourself, "This too shall pass." As Robert Schuller, the late California pastor who was famous for his upbeat, positive messages once said, "Tough times

---

4   https://www.wisefamousquotes.com/shania-twain-quotes/a-friend-is-someone-who-knows-the-song-2196580/

never last, but tough people do."[5] Cry a river, then build a bridge and get over it. You've got work to do!

4. Don't get judgmental; get curious. Rather than responding to negativity by calling it out or by thinking something like, "Wow, this person sure is toxic," ask yourself this question instead: "I wonder what happened to this person that now makes them feel this way?" This is a tactic I use frequently, because it prevents me from becoming too judgmental too quickly. Perhaps the jaded person with whom you are speaking has been seriously wronged by people. Perhaps they have been abandoned or rejected by those closest to them. Perhaps they spent all the previous night in the ICU with a loved one who was at the point of death, and they only managed to get two hours of sleep before their interaction with you. Or as was the case with that jaded 60-something-year-old leader, maybe the person is angry and hurt because his friend has died prematurely and he blames the organization for what happened to him. Do you see them as toxic, now? Or do you see them as people who have been hurt and are not having the healthiest reaction? Perspective changes everything.

5. Find some type of outlet for expressing your frustration and anger, whenever those emotions strike you. I have kept a daily journal since my very first mentor, my principal Lionel Ward, taught me to do so as a fifth grader. Writing is akin to a pressure valve for me; it allows me to let off steam in a productive way. You should not explode with anger whenever you are upset, but you also should not bury it or ignore it, because those bottled-up feelings can easily lead to feelings of jadedness. I don't like to speak using profanity, but boy do I know how to *write* the words! Once I get my emotions on paper, I exhale, smile, and

---

5 Robert H. Schuller, Tough Times Never Last, But Tough People Do! (New York: Bantam Books, 1984).

lock them away from an unsuspecting world. That works for me, though some other form of expression may work better for you. For example, you might bare your soul with a close friend or confidant. You can go to the gym and run your frustrations out on the treadmill. You just want to grab a pillow, place it over your mouth, and scream. If you don't harm another person or yourself, it really doesn't matter what you do. Just find some way to get *out* what is welling up inside of you. Of course, if you still find it difficult to move forward after having tried any of those suggestions, it may be time to sit down with a licensed counselor and explore your feelings a bit more in depth.

6. Learn to assertively confront people who are rude or verbally abusive toward you. I know this may seem counterintuitive, but just stay with me for a moment. I believe one of the reasons we become jaded is because we internalize hurt and pain to the point that it ruins us. Constantly allowing people to "dump on you" eventually wears you down and makes you feel defeated—even helpless.

Many people avoid this type of confrontation because they do not understand the difference between being passive, being aggressive, and being assertive. Allow me to briefly explain:

a)   To be passive is to accept or allow hurtful things to happen to you without responding or resisting;

b)   To be aggressive is to actively seek out confrontation, and even initiate it; but

c)   To be assertive means to confidently and directly speak your mind, calmly, clearly, honestly, and unapologetically.

Passivity and aggression are both extremes, and neither is helpful. The happy medium is *assertiveness*.

Having grown up with what felt like constant verbal abuse, I had to be taught two truths: not only is it essential for our own mental health that we learn to confront those who would verbally demoralize us, but we must also learn how to do so. Here is an assertiveness formula that I have taught many times over the years. I believe you will find it helpful.

Whenever someone is speaking to you in a manner you find offensive, try saying something like this: "When you say/do _____, I feel _____. In the future, _____."

Complete that first blank with the specific behavior the person is exhibiting that you find unacceptable. In the second blank, specifically and honestly tell them how their words/actions make you feel. In the final blank, tell them how you expect them to differently handle situations like this in the future.

Here is an example from one of my clients who used this formula and saw positive results immediately with her cold, insulting father-in-law (she has given me permission to share this): "When you call me 'missy' or 'gal' in front of my children, I feel as if you are purposely trying to humiliate me and disrespect me. I feel as if you think I'm a little child who should be afraid of you. In the future, either call me by my name and speak to me in a respectful tone, or just avoid speaking to me at all." She sent me a direct message one day and said, "Dr. Noble, my father-in-law has decided he will not speak to me. He won't come over anymore if he cannot speak to me however he chooses. And ya' know what—I'm okay with that! Thank you."

She and I both saw this result as a victory and not a failure. While your desire may be to keep your family or extended family intact, the truth is that some relationships are harmful to your mental and physical health. It is neither mean-spirited nor selfish to protect your own well-being. Remaining in toxic relationships is never healthy in the long term. But, if you're not ready to completely sever ties right now, that's okay too. Maybe cutting ties with the plan to reconnect further down the road is the right choice for you. Trust your gut: you'll know when the time is right for you.

7. Make a list of 10 things in your life that you are grateful for or happy about. Focusing on something positive amid experiencing negativity has an amazing way of changing your disposition, thus changing your outcomes.

A few years ago, I was leading a public seminar on customer service for a gathering of business professionals in the San Francisco Bay area. Specifically, I was addressing how to remain positive when having a job that requires you to work with angry, unhappy customers daily. I gave them this same assignment, and told them, "After you make your list of 10, post it in a prominent spot on your wall or your cubicle, and refer to it whenever you find yourself ready to give up on your job—or on your life."

Three weeks after that class, I received an email through my website from one of the attendees. She wrote to me: "Dr. Noble, I must admit that I initially thought that was silly advice, but I tried it anyway, and I owe you an apology—it works! See, I work at a utilities company in the collections department, so I'm getting yelled at and cursed at all day, every day. I referred to that list you had us write, and the number one item on my list was, 'I am grateful for my three wonderful grandkids.' As you suggested when I spoke to you personally in the hallway after your presentation, I brought a picture of my grandkids from home and placed it right beside the telephone. Now, whenever I'm on the phone with an angry customer, I'm looking at my grandbabies at the same time—and I discovered that I can't ever be angry when looking at those angelic faces. Thank you, Dr. Noble—you just saved my career!"

How about you? Are you relatively healthy, even during a global health pandemic? Are you happy with your career? Do you have your basic needs of food and shelter? If you've made mistakes, do you now have the opportunity to correct them? Have you enjoyed your favorite dessert lately? Have you ever overcome a problem you once thought you wouldn't be able to overcome? Your list need not resemble anyone else's; it's as unique as you are. So just make your list, keep it close by, and re-read it whenever you need a reminder of just how good life can be.

8. Spend quality time with those whom you care about and never fail to remind them how important they are to you. I really do not believe that this point needs much explanation. I will simply say that, in your journey of leadership, never be so busy that you fail to spend quality time with those who are with you after the office lights have been turned off. This does not have to be done only with biological family members. Here are just a few suggestions to help you get your own creative juices flowing:

- Regularly plan a monthly family outing together and let different family members choose the spot and/or activity each time. For example, one of you decides they want to go to the waterpark this month. Next month, another decides the group will go out to dinner and movie. The key is to make it a regular date on the calendar that everyone agrees not to miss.

- Schedule dinner time together (or even breakfast time) where everyone agrees to speak to update one another on whatever is going on in their individual lives, with no cell phones or electronic devices allowed at the table.

- Have group reading time, where either everyone listens to one person read from their favorite genre of literature, or where everyone reads something on their own, with everyone making a brief verbal report to the group once everyone is done.

- Record a quick video on your phone or other device and send it to those important people in your life, expressing to them just how much they mean to you.

- Enjoy a hobby together. You could all take a cooking class, ceramics class, or even a spin class together at the gym.[6]

Get creative and make your own list!

9. Be willing to try something new and different. This not only applies to your leadership in the workplace but your life outside the office, as well. Just because XYZ Corporation has always done things in a particular manner does not mean that we should shy away from trying a *different* approach, especially if the tried-and-true approach is losing its potency. A quick way to become jaded is to continue to do the same thing the same way, day after day, month after month, year after year. Shake up your routine, if for no other reason than to prevent yourself from becoming stagnant. As mentioned, you can apply this tip to your personal life, as well. What's keeping you from taking that salsa dance class? Why haven't you tried that new restaurant around the corner yet? Why not jump in the car and take a road trip without really knowing where you're going? Why not just drive until you see something interesting, and then stop? Keeping your life, relationships, and choices fresh is a surefire way to prevent stagnation. And finally:

10. "Don't let people pull you into their storm; pull them into your peace."[7] That quote is attributed to Kimberly Jones, and I wholeheartedly agree with it. Whenever you find yourself in the presence of a jaded person—just as I was with that 60-year-old leader years ago—make a conscious decision to remain positive and refuse to argue. While I *could* have debated with him about his negative comments and spaghetti-filled sabotage, I politely excused myself from the table. I even thanked him for his time. That was not easy

---

6   https://familiesforlife.sg/discover-an-article/pages/30-ways-to-spend-more-family-time.aspx

7   https://www.quotespedia.org/authors/k/kimberly-jones/dont-let-people-pull-you-into-their-storm-pull-them-into-your-peace-kimberly-jones/

to do, but it was essential to maintain my sense of inner peace and calm. Of course, as soon as I got back to my house, I screamed into the pillow, and then I sat down and wrote my true feelings about it in my journal.

Even though I screamed in private and wrote some pretty choice curse words in red ink, I ended the day with my dignity intact. Try it; it works. Confidently excuse yourself from any lunch table that is attempting to serve you a dish of warmed-over cynicism.

In conclusion, you have advantages as a new leader. Not only are you not jaded and have the benefit of not knowing much, but also:

- You are now in a position where you can positively impact the organizational culture for years to come.
- You can help other people grow and develop, which carries with it a profound sense of pride and personal accomplishment when you do it well.
- You have a great opportunity to learn and adapt your personal style of leadership, fine-tuning it along the way.
- You will most likely receive an increase in salary, which isn't a bad thing; and
- Your new leadership position could very well be the first step toward advancing in your career, or—as was the case with me—starting your own business and becoming your own boss. That brings with it a great deal of responsibility, but also a deep sense of freedom and independence that working for someone else seldom affords.

The Possible Pitfalls of Being a New Leader

Just as there are distinct advantages to your new role as a leader, there are some possible pitfalls, too. These can be avoided if you know them and prepare for them. The first pitfall has been alluded to in the previous section:

Timidity In Decision Making

Since repetition is the parent of pedagogy, allow me to say this once again: you are new, and people are *expecting* a certain newness from you. I have read many leadership books that advise new leaders to wait until they get to know everybody on their team and everybody on the board of directors and everybody in the mailroom and all the parking lot attendants before making any changes or decisions. I again repeat I believe this to be bad advice.

When I was a child growing up on the corner of 19th and Marshall Streets in Little Rock, I had a neighbor named Greg. Greg, who I believed to be in his mid to late 20s, had a very, very large dog named—get this—Killer. I, of course, was not the only neighborhood kid who feared Killer, and I avoided him at all costs.

One day as I was walking down the sidewalk, I saw that Greg and Killer were approaching. I immediately panicked and prepared to cross the street to walk on the opposite sidewalk.

Greg, who was a genuinely nice guy despite what I considered to be his rough-and-tumble look and notorious potty-mouth, yelled to me, "Little Noble, he can tell if you're scared. If you don't want him to attack you or bark at you, don't show fear."

I froze in the middle of the street, and slowly began to walk back to the sidewalk I had so hastily left. I stood still, taking deep breaths as Greg and his demon dog approached. I even mustered a smile. Sure enough, Killer came right up to me and stopped.

Greg then said, "Let him lick your hand."

As I gingerly stuck my hand out, this dog from hell licked it. No bite, no bark. I then patted Killer on his head.

Greg smiled at me and said, "Attack dogs can sense your fear, ya know."

I suspect you already perceive the point I'm attempting to make here. Though the people you lead are not vicious attack dogs waiting to chew you to bits, people *can* often sense when you are timid or afraid, and that perception can bring out the worst in them.

Unfortunately, there will be some people who resent you for being in your position, and some people simply will get their jollies by seeking to intimidate you. Though you should not allow any relationship to become adversarial, at the same time, you must understand that you are, in fact, the leader. You deserve to be there, and no amount of huffing and puffing (or barking) should cause you to cower and retreat into the shadows.

Do not be a jerk—but at the same time, do not be timid. You will make some mistakes as a leader, but you will never be able to take the organization to higher heights if you're *afraid* of making a mistake. My high school vice principal Mrs. Othella Faison once said to me, "If you cannot make a mistake, you most likely cannot make anything else happen in your life, either."

I am a huge proponent of positive self-talk. Some define self-talk as that "inner voice that provides a running monologue on [your life] throughout the day."[8] I agree with that definition, and I also add to it by saying sometimes you need to look at yourself in the mirror and say some things aloud to yourself. Tell yourself things like, "I'm intelligent. I'm great at what I do. Today is going to be a wonderful day. I can handle anything that comes my way today." You may feel a bit strange at first, but the more often you say positive things about yourself, the greater your tendency to believe them.

My advice to you is that you learn to tell yourself often: "I'm here, I have earned the right to be here, this will work in my favor, and I can do this. And when I fall, I won't stay down." Muhammad Ali was once asked why he got up so quickly any time he was knocked down in the boxing ring. His response was pure Ali brilliance: "I am a champion, and the floor is no place for a champion."

You, too, are a champion—so don't show your fear, of people, of making mistakes, or of getting back up again.

---

8   https://www.psychologytoday.com/us/basics/self-talk

Allow me to share with you another common pitfall for the emerging leader:

Failing To Understand the Legacy of Your Predecessor (IF you have one)

This point may not apply to you, if yours is a newly created position. However, if you are a new leader replacing an outgoing one, a huge pitfall to avoid is the failure to understand the legacy your predecessor left for you. Whether they realize it or not, every leader leaves a legacy for their successor, and that legacy can be a healthy one or a toxic one. Below are three types of leaders that you may find yourself succeeding:

The Absolute Angel

This is the leader who was revered, admired, and loved, and whose absence the workforce will grieve for a long time. Whether this person retired, died, or was involuntarily replaced, the people who were under their leadership loved them. Be prepared to hear things like, "You've got big shoes to fill, following _____," or, "_____ usually did it THIS way…" No matter how strong of a leader you are or aspire to be, you will never come close to being as good as The Absolute Angel was, as far as these employees are concerned. Nothing you do will be good enough, and when you do get praise, it may only be reluctantly given. But cheer up—you may one day hear them say, "The Absolute Angel was the best leader we've ever had, but you're close behind them!"

We must understand, however, a few facts about The Absolute Angel. In some cases, this person is revered because they were a great leader who empowered and supported those around them—we'll call this one The Good Angel. Yet in other cases, this person is revered because they gave the workforce little accountability and few to no consequences for subpar work performance—we'll call this one The

Bad Angel. Some leaders are loved because they push those on their teams to higher levels of excellence. Others are loved because they let the teams run themselves with little or no input, even when strong leadership is desperately needed.

In my role as an executive leadership coach, I have worked one-on-one with many emerging leaders over the years, some of whom had to follow an Absolute Angel. One executive told me her horrific experience succeeding a Bad Angel. She told me, almost in tears, of how often she was called mean and degrading names because she, unlike her predecessor, was intent upon creating an air of accountability with the team she had just inherited. She lamented the fact that employees had previously been allowed to come consistently late to work. She told me that her predecessor had almost never conducted employee evaluations. She even said that the Bad Angel predecessor would, herself, redo any subpar work for the team rather than setting high expectations of excellence. This new leader's focus upon accountability and professionalism had won her a few friends, but also scores of enemies—and she had only been in the position for about six months.

She told me she wished she had invested in coaching with me prior to things getting to that point, because she had followed that age-old (yet unwise) advice to take it easy for the first few months. Once she finally decided to implement the necessary changes for her team, she was met with criticisms like, "Why are you suddenly being such a [witch] now? You weren't mean like this six months ago!" She took my advice and admitted to her team that she had gotten it wrong by taking things too slowly at the start, but that she had learned from her mistake and would not commit that same error twice. She also told them as per my suggestion, "At the same time, I will never apologize for having exacting standards. The work we do is too important not to be done at the highest levels of excellence."

Within a matter of months, she was receiving some of the highest evaluations in the organization and has since become the third highest ranking member of the management team. She even has a waiting list of employees who want to be transferred to her department. In fact, some of them still call her a "witch," and now they add "...but she and her team produce great results!"

I have also coached emerging leaders who have followed a Good Angel. As you can imagine, the most common question I get from a leader in that situation is, "How do I prove myself and stop all of these comparisons to my predecessor, who apparently walked on water?" First, you will never stop the employees from comparing you to your predecessor. Don't even expect that. However, you can still prove yourself to be a competent, strong leader in the midst of the endless comparisons. Here a just a few tips for doing this:

- **Never, ever badmouth your predecessor.** Whether they were a Good Angel or a Bad Angel, denigrating your predecessor is very unprofessional and almost guarantees that you will never earn the respect you crave.

- **Be deliberate about treating everyone equally well.** Each employee, regardless of their job description, deserves to be treated with dignity and respect. If you cannot or will not treat everyone with the same degree of respect—including those people whose beliefs, backgrounds, or affiliations may be vastly different from your own—then leadership may very well not be for you. Admit that to yourself and move on to some other type of work. Everyone will appreciate it, and so will you.

- **Focus on the right details and keep your team focused on the right details as well.** The next chapter will discuss this matter quite extensively, but for now, just be aware that perhaps the best way to earn respect as a leader is to always keep reminding your team of the main goals, priorities, and details of their work.

- **Clearly explain what it means to be a part of *your* team.** There is a fitting example from the world of professional basketball that I believe is appropriate and helpful here.

There once was a coach named Lenny Wilkens who, at one time, was the winningest coach in NBA history—until another coach, named Phil Jackson, later became the winningest coach. Both were the best of their eras, and each had dramatically different philosophies about how the game should be played. Lenny Wilkens was famous for saying he and he alone determined who played and for how many minutes. In other words, his superstar players never dictated the flow of the game.[9]

- On the other hand, Phil Jackson was well known for entrusting a lot of the on-the-court decision making to his superstar players, like Michael Jordan in Chicago and Kobe Bryant in Los Angeles. And guess what? Both coaching styles worked in their particular settings. Both coaches were effective because they made it very clear to their teams what it meant to be a part of that particular team. This is not simply a basketball story; it's a leadership story. Be clear on your expectations, whatever they may be, and your team is more likely to flourish.

Three keys to earning respect as an emerging leader, despite succeeding the Absolute Angel, are: 1) clear, regular communication on what your expectations are; 2) giving praise when those expectations are met; and 3) immediately following up when those expectations are *not* met.

---

[9] Ed Odeven, Words of wisdom: Coaching advice from Lenny Wilkens, TalkBasket.net. September 8, 2019. https://www.talkbasket.net/44486-words-of-wisdom-coaching-advice-from-lenny-wilkens

It is very possible to do this without having to be an evil tyrant… which leads us to the next type of predecessor you may have to replace:

The Awful Autocrat

This brand of leader follows the motto, "If they fear you, they will follow you." If you have ever had the misfortune of serving under The Awful Autocrat, I commiserate with you. One of my very first supervisors was an Awful Autocrat, and it was the most miserable year-and-a-half I ever spent in my professional career. Suffice it to say, after regular doses of profanity, threats, and insults to everyone on his staff, I secretly applied and was accepted into an extremely competitive and prestigious Ph.D. program. I left without even speaking to my supervisor, though I did inform the HR department. Although I'm not proud of the way I left, if that supervisor's goal was to intimidate to the point that employees were hesitant to talk to him about anything, then mission accomplished.

Most people need to be told "Hey, don't be a jerk." But you're not most people. My suspicion is that one of the reasons you picked up this book is because you are a strong leader whose desire is to be even stronger. So, rather than spending time telling you the issues with *being* an Awful Autocrat, let me instead give you words of advice on successfully *succeeding* one:

- **Give your team the opportunity to vent about their previous experience *without* commentary from you.** Badmouthing your predecessor is never a good idea, even if they happened to have been an Awful Autocrat. However, people who have been subjected to that type of leader need the opportunity to vent and express what they have felt they could not previously express. This can be done in small groups or even a staff meeting, though my personal preference is to do this in one-on-one meetings with each of your direct reports. I recommend doing this one-on-one because it gives you a fantastic opportunity to get to know your employees, plus it helps to create rapport.

While you do not want to chime in with any negative comments you may hear, I do strongly suggest that, after having truly listened to them, you ask them a question like, "So what can I do as your new supervisor to ensure that you don't have that type of experience again?"

That question lets the employee know that you understand the behavior of your predecessor was inappropriate, while also letting them know that you are there to help them heal, move forward, grow, and feel safe. It also lets them know that you will listen to them and are willing to change—two things Autocrats rarely do.

- **Clearly communicate to your team your style of leadership and assure them that they can talk to you about anything.** After having been terrorized by the Awful Autocrat, I'm sure you will understand that many employees may be quite hesitant toward—and even suspicious of— you, even before they get to know you. This is one of those areas where the adage rings true: "Time heals all wounds." Give them the time they need to unpack their emotional/ psychological baggage, and do not take their distrust of you personally. It's not about you; it's about the residue left behind by your predecessor.

You can help start the healing process by letting them know your leadership style is quite different than what they have just experienced. In fact, you don't even have to say, "I won't be like your last leader." For example, instead of telling them, "I don't mind if you leave a few minutes early to pick up kids from school," put your money where your mouth is: when you see a parent packing up or asking if they can head out, allow them to do so and give them a smile. Actions speak louder than words! Rather than tell them who you are *not*, show them who you *are*. They will connect the dots and say to themselves, "Wow, this leader sounds nothing like that last one. Thank God!"

The Aloof Apathetic

Have you ever known anyone who had been on their job for so long and had enjoyed their job so little that their last few years on the job were spent doing little work and doing lots of daydreaming (usually about retirement at a tropical location)? Everybody, meet the third type of predecessor: The Aloof Apathetic. A surefire way to recognize an Aloof Apathetic is their usage of the word "they" instead of the word "we." If you ask this person of any new developments on the job, they may very well respond with, "They've been doing a lot of XYZ lately," or even, "I don't know what they are doing here." This person is the one who was simply biding their time until retirement. They didn't want much responsibility; in fact, they may have dumped all their responsibility on others (there is a huge difference between delegating and dumping, which I will share with you in Chapter 4).

Do not be at all surprised if, as you succeed this leader, you find a department or a team in complete disarray and drowning in discouragement. Those employees had the great misfortune of having had a leader who no longer cared about whether the job got done at all, let alone caring about the quality of work that was produced. What the employees will need from you are some of the same needs they will have no matter who you are succeeding:

- **You must help the team to focus on the right details of their work.**
- **Clearly explain to your team why work quality is important to you and to the organization.**
- **You should clearly explain what it means to be a player on your team now, including why aloofness is not part of**

who you are and why you will not allow it from anyone on your team, and

- **You should give them opportunities to vent about their previous experience.**

All the while, remember never to badmouth your predecessor, no matter who they were.

Here is an opportunity for you to be creative and help me write even more content for this book: can you think of any other types of predecessors that I did not mention? Is there a fourth or a fifth type that you can think of? I have provided space for you to explore this question further in the third implementation task found at the end of this chapter.

While we could certainly list more pitfalls to avoid, the final one I will share with you is this:

Failing To Ask the Right Questions of Your Supervisor

Your first few days or weeks in your new position will be a time of information gathering, and a key informational conversation you will need to have will be a conversation with your immediate supervisor. This conversation or series of conversations will be essential to getting the strongest start possible. It is not a good sign when a leader asks a new or prospective employee, "Do you have any questions?" and the answer is, "No." Asking questions of your new supervisor gives you the opportunity to learn more about your new position. It also shows that you have done some research and have given some thoughtful reflection to this new endeavor. So, I will now share with you essential questions any emerging leader must ask their immediate supervisor. Starting with…

"How Do You Prefer I Communicate With You?"

I once had a supervisor who always kept his office door open. I incorrectly assumed that his open door meant, "Come on in if you need to." I quickly learned, by his often terse and exasperated responses, that his open door simply meant, "The air conditioning unit in this old building needs to be replaced, and I'm hot." When he finally told me it bothered him, I quickly wised up, apologized for my past intrusions, and asked him, "How do you prefer I communicate with you?"

He was a genuinely nice person, and he said to me, "I'm the type of person who prefers to talk on the run. If you happen to see me walking across the campus, that's the best time to talk to me. Let's talk as we walk. Thanks for asking." This is definitely not every supervisor's preference, which is why it is important to ask. In fact, he is the only supervisor I ever had who preferred that type of communication.

Let my hard-way lesson be of help to you. Be sure to ask your supervisor, preferably the very first time you meet with them, their preferred method of communication. Some supervisors will indeed have an open-door policy, which means you should come in whenever you can. Others will prefer that you make an appointment first, either via email or telephone. Does your supervisor prefer face-to-face communication, or texting? Does your supervisor prefer verbal reports, or are formal, written reports more to their liking? Their preference is not as important as your adapting your communication to their preference. If you begin the relationship with poor communication, things may go downhill from there. As the saying goes, you never get a second chance to make a first impression.

Also, ask your supervisor how often they wish to meet with you and/or hear from you. You will never know, otherwise, if you're bothering them or keeping them too much in the dark. You don't want to be a pest, but you also do not want to be accused of not communicating enough. Don't guess or assume—ask.

Keep in mind that you too are a leader now, so please be intentional about communicating your expectations to those whom you lead. Answer this same question for your employees. How do you prefer they communicate with you? Don't assume they know what your preferences are, and don't wait for them to come ask you. Remember, your responsibility as the coach is to make clear to everyone what it will be like to play on your team.

"What Do You See As My Most Challenging Task?"

Asking this question is an amazingly effective way of learning the problems within the organization, the problems within your department, or the problems on the specific team to which you will now give leadership. You may hear your supervisor say, "You know, I think your biggest issue will be getting them to trust you, since you're new." Or you might hear something like this: "I think your greatest challenge will be getting them motivated. Many of them seem to be simply marking time. I would like to see you help them ramp up their enthusiasm."

Whatever you hear, realize that your supervisor's answer will be a great window into your new position and expectations.

"What do you see as my top priority?"

If your priorities do not line up with your supervisor's, you are headed for trouble. While you may think the most important task is organizing a staff retreat so you can explain to the team your vision for the organization, your supervisor's top priority may be getting your team out of the habit of turning their reports in after the deadline. In this scenario, your priority might directly take away from your supervisor's!

Never assume that you and your supervisor are on the same page concerning priorities. Ask them what they see as your top priority and begin to tackle that first. Yes, you're new, so you are expected to make some changes. At the same time, you must also keep in mind that you must fit into the company culture and the role for which they hired you. So, make sure you ask your supervisor what they see as the first leadership issue you should address. By doing this, you can score an early win which will not only please your supervisor but will boost your confidence as well, creating great momentum for you as you move forward in leadership. It's critical to get an early win under your belt, and asking this question is a great step towards making that happen for you.

Wrap-up

Okay, it's time to take a deep breath and reflect on what you have learned so far. You now know:

- The many advantages of being a new leader.
- How to be proactive and avoid becoming jaded in your later years of leadership.
- How to be more assertive without being aggressive.
- How to avoid the common pitfalls of newness.
- How to deal with the legacy of your predecessor.
- How to demonstrate who you really are to the people you now lead (and remember - actions speak louder than words); and
- The most important questions to ask your supervisor and why those questions are so important.

But what if you find yourself a bit overwhelmed by all your new responsibilities, and it becomes difficult for you to know which issues to tackle first? What if, even after figuring out your supervisor's priorities, you are yet unsure of what your first steps should be as the new leader? What if you find yourself leading a team of unmotivated people who are simply going through the motions, punching a time clock, and, in a sense, phoning it in? Don't worry--in chapter two, we are going to cover exactly how to focus on the *right* details so you can nip all those problems in the bud.

Chapter 1 Implementation Tasks:

1. Decide which of the 10 tips to avoid jadedness are most applicable to you, and immediately begin to implement them.
2. Decide if there is anyone with whom you need to be more assertive, and then begin to practice using the assertiveness formula to prepare for your conversation with them. Find a friend who is willing to role play with you to give you some practice before that conversation occurs; you will be yourself and your friend will play the role of the person you plan to confront.
3. Determine which category your predecessor falls into, or even produce your own 4th or 5th type of predecessor that we did not cover in this chapter. Then, take the suggested steps to successfully handle that legacy.
4. Make an appointment with your supervisor and ask them these three essential questions:
    1. *"How do you prefer I communicate with you?"*
    2. *"What do you see as my most challenging task?"*
    3. *"What do you see as my top priority?"*

Chapter 1 Reactions:

1. What did I already know?

2. Of what was I reminded? How will I act upon those reminders?

3. What was brand new information for me?

Focusing On The Right Details

"That's been one of my mantras - focus and simplicity. Simple can be harder than complex: You have to work hard to get your thinking clean to make it simple. But it's worth it in the end because once you get there, you can move mountains." – Steve Jobs[10]

Every great leader wants to move mountains. We all have an unquenchable desire to be known for having made a permanent, positive impact. And yet, this type of greatness only comes to a few leaders. The difference between the leaders who go on to become heroes and the leaders who are forgotten the moment they leave the company is that the greatest leaders know how to focus on the right *details*, whatever those details may be. This brings a few questions to the forefront:

1. What right details are worthy of my laser-like focus as a leader?
2. Why are these details critical to my success as a leader?
3. More importantly, why are these details critical to the success of the team, group, or department I lead?

---

[10] https://www.brainyquote.com/authors/steve-jobs-quotes

We will answer all these questions in turn, but let's start with the first. I propose that the details that are most worthy of your laser-like focus are the *decisions* you will inevitably make as a leader—many of which will occur daily. Perhaps nothing else has such enormous potential to make or break you as a leader as your ability to make the right decisions at the right time in the right manner.

The Importance Of Making Decisions As A Leader

Leaders regularly make decisions that impact all aspects of the organization—employees, clients, potential clients, financials, and so on. Leaders must be able to judge quickly and effectively what is best for the organization and everyone the organization serves. Correct decisions can yield positive results from repeat customers, leading to increased financial strength and a healthy work environment where employees regularly give their best efforts. On the other hand, poor decisions, though not necessarily fatal, can impede progress in significant ways.

But why does the thought of having to make decisions frighten so many leaders? Psychologist Michelle P. Maidenberg suggests the following reasons:

"Decision-making requires us to take risks and give up a degree of control because of uncertainty. There is usually a tradeoff that we must accept for making the decision we choose. We tend to be fearful of making a poor decision and it being deemed or reinforced that we failed and are therefore a failure. We also worry about the potential rippling effects that we think we may not be able to reconcile."[11]

---

[11] Michelle P. Maidenberg, "6 Tips for Making Difficult Decisions," Psychology Today, March 16, 2021, Retrieved from https://libguides.heidelberg.edu/chicago/article#:~:text=Footnote%2FEndnote&text=Last%20Name%2C%20%22Article%20Title%2C,necessary)%2C%22%20page%20cited.

Given the importance of decision-making, the ability to discern *which* decisions to focus upon is a key characteristic of an effective leader. In this chapter, I suggest for you the five decisions below, which I believe are most worthy of the focus of leaders in general— and of emerging leaders in particular:

1. Decide upon the direction and the destination of the organization and its employees.
2. Decide to be the chief motivator of your team.
3. Decide what each team member needs most from you. (Hint: they do *not* each need the exact same thing from you.)
4. Decide how to prioritize your daily schedule in order to maximize effectiveness.
5. Decide to be the type of leader others want to follow.

Let's dive more deeply into how to best make these decisions. As I discuss each one, I will also explain why these decisions are worthy of special focus and how focusing upon them will exponentially increase your potential for success as a new leader.

Decide Upon the Direction and the Destination of the Organization and its Employees

I want you to imagine you are on an airplane heading for a vacation you have been carefully planning for quite some time. The cabin doors have finally closed, and the journey is about to begin. Just before you take off, the pilot comes on over the loudspeaker and says, "Ladies and gentlemen, welcome to flight 3353. I am your pilot. Um…I have no idea where we're going but trust me when I tell you I'll get you there. Fasten your seat belts."

Chances are you would be trying to get off that airplane immediately, and I don't blame you. You would not have any confidence in that pilot's ability, because that pilot was not clear about where they were trying to take you. We expect our pilots to know not only where we're going, but to know how to get us there. And if the pilot is not clear, the people are going to panic.

As a leader, I want you to think of yourself as the pilot. If you do not have a clear idea of where you're trying to take this organization, the people you lead are going to be confused and, most likely, they're going to enter a state of panic.

It may not be fair, but it is true: when a team is underperforming, you look to the leader. What typically happens when a sports team has a string of losing seasons? The first move the front office usually makes is to fire the coach. Now that may not be fair in your estimation, but it is true that, chances are, there is something wrong with the team's leadership.

There are three navigational questions you need to ask if you're going to be an effective leader who takes the people you lead in the direction they should go. These questions begin and end with you because everything rises and falls with leadership. These are not questions you need to ask of your people; these are questions you need to ask of yourself, and they should be answered in order. The first question is:

1. What is my purpose as the leader? In other words, what do I do as leader? If you were talking to someone who knew absolutely nothing about your industry, role, or product or service, how would you describe what you do in one sentence?

"As the leader of XYZ Organization, my job is to_____."

I have done this exercise with leaders all around the globe, and you would be surprised how many leaders cannot simply and succinctly describe what it is they're supposed to do.

Folks, if you are the pilot and you do not know what you're doing or where you're going, your airplane is headed for major turbulence. If your leadership is fuzzy, the people who are following you, who are looking to you for guidance and direction, will feel even more lost in the fog than you do. So, the first question you need to answer is, "What am I supposed to be accomplishing as the leader of this organization? What do I do? Where am I leading this company? And how can I explain that in one simple sentence?" If you can explain it that way, that means you're clear about your job, your goals for the company, and how you're working to get to your destination.

2. What is the purpose of this department/team/group that I'm leading? Let's say, for example, you are the director of human resources. Your next question is, *what does the human resources department do?* Do you have an answer to that question already? If so, place it right here:

> *The purpose of the _____ department/*
> *division/team, which I now lead,*
> *is to_____.*

Now, you can tie the first two questions together: "What do I do as director that helps human resources do what it does?" By doing this, you'll begin to form a clearer picture of your purpose within the company.

Of course, if your position is the president or CEO, you may not have an individual department or group that you lead, so you may skip this second question and move on to the third question. This third question is for everybody.

3. What is the purpose of this organization as a whole? As a leader, you've got to be crystal clear. Do not use code words. Do not use jargon. Explain your company to somebody who knows absolutely nothing about it. Again, use one sentence:

> *The purpose of the XYZ Organization is to_____.*

Let's say you work for XYZ company; and within XYZ company, you are the director of human resources. You now have three levels of questions you need to ask and answer: *"What do I do as human resources director that helps the human resources department do what it does? How does that help XYZ company do what it does?"*

As the leader, you need to be able to clearly articulate what you do that helps your department do what the organization is supposed to do. Those are the three levels of understanding when it comes to leadership. If you cannot clearly articulate answers to each of those, you are just like that pilot who gets on the plane and says, "I'm taking you somewhere. Don't ask me where—just trust me."

After you answer these three questions for yourself, it becomes your responsibility to make sure each one of your employees has an answer to the same questions for *themselves*: *"What do I as (job title) that helps (department name) do what (XYZ Organization) does?"*

Remember leader, *you* are the pilot, and the direction and safe arrival of the aircraft and its precious human cargo is in your hands. Everything rises and falls with leadership. If the team is unclear about its direction and purpose, I'm not talking to the team first—I'm coming straight for the leader. Why? Because those you lead cannot answer those questions for *themselves* until you first answer those questions for *yourself.*

By now, you have made this first crucial decision of who you are and where you are taking this organization. Next up, we need to get the people in this organization on your side.

Decide To Be the Chief Motivator for Your Team.

You may find yourself leading a team of people who are only here to collect a paycheck—just phoning it in, so to speak. How do you get these people motivated and excited about their work? Here is the answer: you must connect them to the higher purpose of their job. In other words, you must help them to understand the "why" behind what they do. If they don't have a good, strong reason why they do what they do, if they don't have a compelling answer as to why their job is important, they're probably not going to do their job with much enthusiasm or energy.

Nothing motivates more than understanding the true purpose of a job. Plus, nothing will make your team as a whole gel together more quickly than understanding their collective purpose as a team.

Allow me to illustrate this point by sharing with you a true experience I had. Several years ago, I was called upon to conduct some skills training for a school district in Northern California. The superintendent of the school district called me during the summer and said, "Dr. Noble, I need you to conduct some training for our employees before the school year begins. Specifically, I need you to conduct some training for our cafeteria workers. At the end of last school year, we did a survey and we discovered that everybody hates our cafeteria ladies. When it comes time to go to lunch, the children start crying. They do not want to go to the cafeteria because these cafeteria ladies are so mean! They scare these poor kids. They yell and scream at them things like, 'Sit down! Shut up! Eat your food!' I mean, Dr. Noble, the kids are scared to death. We need you, before the school year starts, to take these cafeteria workers and turn them into a kinder, gentler group of food service workers. Can you do that?"

Of course, I said, "Sure. I could do that." But I was thinking to myself, *How in the world am I going to do that in one seven-hour day?*

I arrived on the day of training at a big, downtown hotel ballroom filled with cafeteria workers. I had a daunting task ahead of me—then, a sudden flash of inspiration hit. I begin the day of training by asking this question: "Ladies, can one of you tell me what you do, in one simple sentence of 20 words or fewer? What's your job?"

That question should sound familiar to you.

In response to that question, one of the ladies stood up and, dripping with attitude, said, "You wanna know what we do every day? Okay, I'll tell ya. We slap square pizza, mashed potatoes, and corn on each tray, and we give it to kids. Can we go now?"

Oh, I love a challenge. I mused to myself, "I've got my work cut out for me today."

I began to zero in on her terse response. "Okay, ladies, how many of you realize that the children who get free lunch at school receive that free lunch because their families cannot afford to feed them healthy, nutritious meals every day? How many of you realize that these kids get lunch because they don't always get the right food at home?"

All the cafeteria ladies raised their hands. I expected that; there was a method to my madness. The first thing I knew I needed to do was create consensus about the higher purpose of the job this group of frustrated cafeteria ladies (who very obviously did not want to be there with me that day) shared. If you're going to get a group of workers to come together for a higher purpose, you've got to make sure they all have that clear purpose in common. They all raised their hands in agreement and several even verbalized their agreement. They all agreed that those children were receiving lunch in the cafeterias because their parents could not necessarily afford to give them good meals.

I then said, "Okay, now that we agree upon that, how many of you realize that if a child does not have a good, healthy meal, they may exhibit some behavioral problems?"

That is where the mood really shifted, and the cafeteria ladies became almost immediately animated.

"That's the problem with these kids," one said. "These kids are eating doughnuts and sugary cereal and candy bars for breakfast. By the time they come to school, they're all hopped up and high on sugar; and by the time they come to us in the cafeteria, they're bouncing off the walls. So, we have to yell, we have to scream, we have to say, 'sit down and shut up.' You're absolutely right—if these kids ate better breakfasts, they would be better behaved before lunchtime."

This part of the conversation continued for almost one full hour. They got excited and several of them began to chime in with comments such as, "Dr. Noble, thank God you're here. The district officials need to hear this conversation we're having right now."

I eventually said, "If these children were better behaved because they were better nourished, how would that make your jobs more enjoyable?"

"Well, we wouldn't have to scream so much," one said. "We wouldn't have to yell. I wouldn't be so stressed out."

Another cafeteria worker said, "Not only that, but if these kids behaved themselves, they could pay better attention in the classrooms. They could grow up to be model citizens. And as I become a *senior* citizen, I wouldn't have any worries about these kids taking over the world."

After more than 60 minutes of intense discussion and loud agreement that almost made me feel as if I were leading a tent revival meeting, I said, "Okay, ladies, let's go back full circle. Can somebody here tell me what you do, in one sentence?"

Now remember, the first answer to that question was something about slapping square pizza, mashed potatoes, and corn onto a tray. But this time, the *same* lady responded: "Dr. Noble, we provide healthy, nutritious food for children so they can behave themselves properly and grow up to be responsible citizens."

Boom!

Those cafeteria ladies moved from describing their life's work as slapping around square pizza to providing nutritious, healthy food for children so they can grow up to be model citizens. If your idea of your job is simply slapping square pizza, mashed potatoes, and corn onto a tray, you're probably not going to do your job with much enthusiasm, or care about solving the problems you encounter. What I helped those food service workers to do that day was understand the higher purpose behind their job. This helped them feel better about their careers and even want to improve them.

Those food service workers finally understood their purpose: to provide healthy food for these children. But that's not the end of the story—it was only the beginning. I kid you not: the following month, after the training was over, I received another phone call from the district superintendent, the same person who had hired me in the first place.

In a rather abrupt voice, he said to me, "Dr. Noble, what did you do to the cafeteria ladies last month?"

I started to panic. I said to myself, "Uh oh, what did I do wrong? Did I offend somebody? Had I used some off-color language, or something?"

I replied to the superintendent, "What do you mean what did I do to the cafeteria ladies?"

He said, "Dr. Noble, we have had to start opening the school buildings earlier. The cafeteria workers insist on getting there early to get a jumpstart on cooking better lunches. Secondly, all the cafeteria ladies got together and wrote a letter, signed it —each of them—and sent the letter to the school district office *demanding* we start a free breakfast program. The letter said, in part, '…breakfast is the most important meal of the day, and when these children don't eat proper breakfast; it creates behavioral problems. So, we need to start them off the right way. Instead of sugar and donuts and candy bars, we need to give them a healthy breakfast in the morning.'"

The superintendent added, "Dr. Noble, here's the kicker: not one of them asked for a raise. They're willing to come in early. They're willing to cook an extra meal and none of them demanded more money. Dr. Noble, what did you do?"

And I said to him, "I helped them understand the deeper purpose behind their job. And once they realized that their purpose was bigger than square pizza, mashed potatoes, and corn, that realization provided an *inner motivation*. They motivated themselves because they had a higher purpose."

Self-motivation is the most powerful motivation available.

The postscript to this story is that the cafeteria workers did end up getting their breakfast program—and they also got a raise, which they deserve. To this day, I continue to be their trainer every year before the school year starts.

I want you to take this lesson with you and apply it wherever you need it. As the leader, you must decide to be the chief motivator of your team, and the best way to provide that motivation is to help your team unlock self-motivation by clarifying the greater purpose behind their job. Having a greater sense of purpose creates more lasting motivation than money ever will—though your employees do deserve to be well paid for their expertise. Some leaders and organizations erroneously think that simply throwing money at their workers will help motivate them to work harder, but nothing could be further from the truth. If you want a team that motivates themselves and decides within themselves to work harder and always give their best, you as their leader must help them discover a greater purpose than square pizza, mashed potatoes, and corn.

Before I leave this point, I will give you one more example of this phenomenon from a group coaching session I conducted. I was speaking about discovering the greater purpose of your job, and one exasperated gentleman said, "Doc, I want to believe what you're saying—I really do, but in my case I can't. I just don't see any deep, high purpose for my job."

I asked him, "Well do you mind if I ask your colleagues here this morning to listen as you share your story, and then chime in with their interpretations? Perhaps that will help you."

He responded sullenly, "Okay, I guess. But, as I said, there is not a high purpose for me. I just own a party goods store. I sell party hats, party favors, balloons, candles, streamers, decorations, blah blah blah."

I must say that I was so proud of the attendees that morning. They had learned the lesson and were now about to help their colleague.

One of the attendees said to him, "So you own a party store, huh? What types of parties do people have that require them to come shop with you?"

The gentleman responded, "Well, people come to buy supplies for everything from birthday parties to weddings to bar mitzvahs to quinceaneras."

I could see the attendees smiling and getting excited, because they could see where the conversation was going. One of them grinned from ear to ear and said in a manner that I can only describe as lovingly sarcastic, "Hmmmm, weddings, birthdays, graduations... sounds like some pretty special occasions are being celebrated. Occasions that bring families and friends together to see one another, laugh with one another, express their love and pride to one another. And they come to *you* to help them with that, huh?"

The silence hung in the air for what seemed like an eternity. The gentleman who had said there was no purpose to his work finally said, "Okay, I get it. So, I don't just sell hats and balloons and candles...I make it possible for families and friends to come together and celebrate major milestones with one another!" Finally, he smiled. "Now that's something worth waking up for!"

Get the point? As the leader, you have the responsibility to ensure each employee can articulate the same type of purposeful description of the work they do. Sounds like you now have a homework assignment, huh?

Decide to learn what each team member needs most from you.

One of my desires for you, emerging leader, is that you learn more quickly than I did that one-size-fits-all might be great for athletic wear, but it can be a disastrous approach when it comes to leading people. Not every person you lead will need the same type of attention from you, and there is no single approach to leadership that can be applied across the board to every person.

People are different. They have different backgrounds, different personalities, different ideas of right and wrong, and different work ethics. Therefore, it is incumbent upon you as the leader to skillfully determine who needs what, when they need it, and why. As I often say, you cannot lead them if you do not know them.

Years ago, I attended a Little League baseball game. A good friend of mine was coaching one of the teams, and he had invited me to come watch one of their championship tournaments games. Midway through, my friend, the coach, pulled one of his young ball players aside, looked him right in the eyes, and said in his stern coach persona, "Come on, kid; get your head in the game. Focus!"

The young athlete responded enthusiastically, "Got it, coach!"

Then my friend pulled another young athlete to the side, looked him right in the eyes, and said the exact same words in the exact same tone: "Come on kid; get your head in the game. Focus!"

That young athlete's response was quite different: he began to cry uncontrollably. He wailed through his tears, "Why are you always yelling at me? Why don't you like me?"

Of course, some people might read that account and conclude, "That's the kid's fault. He was obviously too sensitive. He wasn't tough enough. There's no crying in baseball!" I disagree that the scenario played out the way it did because the kid was "soft." On the contrary, it provides an excellent opportunity for the coach to recognize and appreciate the differences between the players on the team without making quick, rash judgments about them. If I know I have a crier on the team, it would be more helpful to get curious and ask myself, "I wonder why they're crying? Is it because they are used to being told they don't measure up? Is my physical size intimidating to them?" You might even end up saying to the player: "I do like you, and I apologize for making you feel like I don't." Perhaps that type of reassurance is all they needed in the first place. Becoming curious instead of judgmental provides an excellent opportunity to get to know the player better and give them the type of coaching they need so that they can eventually fit into your system.

When it comes to leadership, one size does not fit all. As the leader, as the coach, as the chief motivator, it is your responsibility to know each one of your players well. What do they need most from you? What is the best way to speak to them? What should you never say to them? What are their biggest fears or insecurities? How do they wish to be rewarded for a job well done? You cannot learn about the people you lead by sitting in your office all day every day, waiting to be needed.

If you cannot answer those basic questions about each one of the people you lead, your next homework assignment is to get out of your office and get to know your people. This may mean taking each one of them out to lunch; it may mean having a one-on-one with each of them and directly asking them those questions; it may mean intensely observing them as they do their job and quietly making notes for yourself. Whatever you do, get to know them so you can effectively lead them.

One of the most important decisions for you to make as a leader is to decide to learn what each of your team members needs most from you to maximize their effectiveness on the job. Individualized coaching not only helps keep you mindful of the fact that a team is composed of various individuals who must work together for a common goal, but it also opens the door for you to create an individualized growth plan for each of the people you lead. To be effective, those individual growth plans must first take into consideration the strengths and weaknesses of each of your team members. There are two essential qualities that an employee must have, for them to be a valuable member of your team. It will be your responsibility to assess how strong or how weak those two traits are for each of your team members. And it is also your responsibility to learn how to bring out the best in each of them. After all, that is the very definition of a good coach. Let's now explore this further.

If an employee is going to be a valuable member of your team, add to the bottom line, and make sure that the workplace is productive and enjoyable, they must possess two qualities in abundance:

1. Exceptional *ability*. Ability simply means possession of the means or skill to do something. In other words, can this person skillfully execute their job duties? Are they good at what they do? If the person is a custodian, are the facilities consistently clean? If the person is an accountant, are they excellent with numbers and figures? Here are just a few ways to determine if someone is good at their job, even if you are unfamiliar with their job responsibilities:

- Observe them as they do their work and watch how smoothly they function. Are they easily frazzled or frustrated, or do they seem comfortable in the execution of their duties?
- Read their past evaluations and see if you notice consistent compliments and positive remarks about their job performance.
- Talk to others in the organization whose work is affected by this employee's performance. For example, if the employee is the payroll clerk, ask others within the organization if they always get paid on time or if they often experience issues with their pay. If the employee is the staff accountant, ask others in the organization if they consistently receive (with a high degree of accuracy) all the facts, figures, and financial reports they need from the accountant to perform their own duties in a timely manner.

2. Exceptional *attitude*. This is a bit less tangible, but just as important. While "ability" means whether or not they can do the job well, "attitude" is their mindset *while* they're doing the job. Are they easy to get along with? Do they take direction and instruction very well? Do they create drama with their coworkers? Are they willing to learn? If they don't know something, are they willing to admit it—and are they willing to be taught?

A great employee will possess both great ability and a great attitude. They must have both if they're going to be a superstar on your team.

Do you know that type of employee that makes their coworkers silently rejoice when they hear they got sick? You cannot afford to have those types of employees on your team. You and I both know that if you tolerate a bad employee, you will end up killing the morale of all your good employees. You must make sure your employees have both the ability and the attitude needed.

Let's discuss the four types of employees you will find yourself leading, based on their possession or lack thereof of these two basic qualities of ability and attitude. [12]

- Great ability and great attitude (The Superstar).
- Great ability, poor attitude (The Disgruntled).
- Great attitude, poor ability (The Go-Getter); and
- Poor attitude, poor ability (The Poison).

It's important to learn these types well, because each of them needs something different from you as their leader. Before diving in, I want you to do this homework assignment: make a list of every employee you supervise. If you supervise many employees, narrow it down to the employees who might need the most help from you. As you read, categorize your employees according to the four employee types. By the end of this, you'll have a good idea of what each member of your team needs from you (although, asking them directly is never a bad idea!). Let's look at each category more closely and see what they need in order to maximize their effectiveness.

1. The Superstar - Great ability and great attitude. This person performs their job duties exceptionally well—and on top of that, they also get along well with others, work well with others, and take instruction and constructive criticism well. They're willing to learn, and they're even willing to improve. These are your Superstars.

Superstar employees are the people you can trust to help you train other employees—or even to handle the training themselves

---

[12] In 1968, Bruce Henderson, the founder of the Boston Consulting Group (BCG), created what he dubbed the BCG Matrix as a way of helping companies identify where to invest their resources. It became wildly popular in the business world and, because of its immense popularity, human resource departments adapted it and started to apply a similar matrix to the process of employee evaluation. It has since appeared in many different formats worldwide. What I include here is my own variation of this matrix.

without micromanagement needed. They are already good at what they do, and they already have a great attitude; that's what makes them Superstars. However, just like a star athlete, there are drawbacks. If a Superstar sits on the bench too long or doesn't feel appropriately recognized/rewarded for their efforts, they will either revert to their old ways before they became a Superstar, or in other words, they will employ what I call the LeBron James technique: "I'm taking my talents elsewhere."

People need to go where they're appreciated, not simply tolerated. If you have somebody on your team who has both a great attitude and great ability, you need to appreciate them and use them to their full ability. Start by giving them more responsibility—allow them to partner with you to train their coworkers.

Superstars do not need as much access to you as their colleagues might. That does not mean that you should never meet with them one-on-one; it simply means that they do not need as much hands-on mentoring. That frees you up to spend more time with those who need more help from you.

Right now, the Superstar is the ONLY employee who is ready for you to delegate more responsibility to them—but more on delegation in chapter 4.

2. The Disgruntled - Great ability, bad attitude. This person is not necessarily somebody you want to fire. Rather, bring them into your office so they can have a one-on-one conversation with you. This person is not someone who is intentionally causing harm or deliberately creating trouble, like angry outbursts, or intentionally spreading lies. This person typically can be recognized by the fact that they seem to now pull away from the group where they once were more actively involved in group discussions, project planning, or activities.

You need to figure out why this person with great ability has a bad attitude. Maybe they have a bad attitude because they're being bullied by one of their coworkers. Perhaps they have a bad attitude because they've been passed up for promotions in the past and they're bitter about it. Whatever the case may be, you need to discover the root of the attitude problem. Once you do—and fix it—the disgruntled usually moves to the category of superstar.

3. The Go-Getter - Great attitude, poor ability. This person needs training from you because they *could* eventually be good at their job. Now, they just don't know how to do their job well. The best part is, when you tell a go-getter, "Hey, I'm going to send you to some training," or, "I'm going to bring Dr. Noble in to spend some time with you," or, "I'm going to assign your [superstar] colleague to teach you everything they know," the Go-Getter gets excited, because they have a great attitude! They want to learn; they want to improve; they realize they're not very good at the job. The fact you said you want them on your team enough that you're going to give them some training gets them excited. They can be taught a skillset that will eventually move them to the category of superstar: great attitude and great ability.

Are you beginning to see that the goal of this entire process is to move everybody to that category of superstar? That's your job as the leader, to build a team of stars.

But there's a fourth and final category:

4. The Poison - Poor attitude and poor ability. I am open to suggestions for a better, more humane term, but for now, the word "poison" does describe the effect this person has on your team. The major differences between a Disgruntled and a Poison is that a Poison is usually a bit more deliberate and even aggressive in their behaviors. While a Disgruntled typically pulls away from the group, a Poison interjects themselves even more into the group dynamic to cause disruption or sow seeds of discord. They don't get along with people, they create drama in the workplace, and very often nobody wants to work with them. Plus, they're not even that good at their job!

Let me ask you a simple question about employees in this category: why do they still have a job with you in the first place? Maybe they're the boss' child, or they have tenure, or they are very sick and grumpy but used to be a Superstar before they got sick. Maybe they're grieving a recent loss or dealing with mental illness. Maybe they're your best friend from high school. Unless you have an excellent rapport with your boss, removing the boss' child may not even be an option. If the person is dealing with grief of some sort, then perhaps offering days off for mental wellness would be a helpful route to take. If the person was once a Superstar and has fallen out of grace, they are now in the Disgruntled category and need a one-on-one with you.

As you can see, some of these issues are worth waiting out or trying to fix, while some very simply are not. If this person responds to your implemented solutions, like the ones I discussed above, then you can eventually move them out of the Poison category.

I believe each employee regardless of their issues can be rehabbed or improved. But this final category is the only category that includes some people I would choose to fire. I typically do not want to terminate people. I'm a teacher and coach at heart, so I want to train people (Go-getters), have one-on-ones with people (Disgruntled), or give them more responsibility (Superstars). But the only person I ever consider firing is the person with the bad attitude and the bad ability whose issue is not worth waiting out or attempting to fix. If they can't do the job and their attitude stinks, they have no place on my team.

What's worse is that if I don't get rid of them, they are going to kill the morale of the other people on the team. That's what poison does. A little poison goes a long way in destroying a healthy body. Therefore, because I want a healthy body, I don't negotiate with poison that cannot be fixed. *I remove it.*

Look at the people you placed into that category and ask yourself, "Why are they still on my payroll?"

If you decide to keep this person on your team, you need to be ready to explain to the rest of the team why you are allowing this person to remain. I will now tell you something that you have probably already figured out: your team will begin to resent you as their leader if you continue to tolerate poison in the ranks. Why is this person allowed to remain without changing or improving? That's the question you must answer for yourself. I can't answer that one for you, but I can help you ask the question.

Kate Ashford, contributing writer to Monster.com, suggests there are at least six ways to handle poisonous employees, whom she describes as toxic. They are:

- Have a discussion with them in private. This will help you to determine if the person is dealing with a larger issue than can be fixed or if they are simply not a good fit for you and the organization.
- Be prepared for pushback. Expect the employee to debate and even argue with you about your findings.
- Document everything. This is sage advice, even if you're not dealing with a Poison. Ashford specifically suggests: "Keep a record of the employee's activities that you believe are disruptive. Refer to this list when you meet with the employee to discuss their performance. Pointing out specific examples may help them recognize types of behaviors that they don't even realize they're exhibiting."
- Offer constructive feedback in public. If this person's disruptive behavior occurs in a group setting, such as a staff meeting, then you should address their behavior specifically and immediately in that same setting. Letting it slide sends the wrong message to your team, and that message is that you are willing to tolerate toxic behavior.
- Comment on the behavior, not the person's character. For example, instead of responding to a negative comment with "You are really being negative right now,' respond instead with "That comment comes across as rather negative. Rephrase it, please."
- Continue to grow as a leader. Dealing with a toxic employee will not be the only challenge you ever face in leadership,

so commit yourself to reading books such as this one and seek out advice from leaders whose opinions you respect.[13]

So, to recap, here is what each employee needs from you if your plan is to create a team filled with Superstars:

- Great ability, great attitude (The Superstar) - they need more responsibility.
- Great ability, poor attitude (The Disgruntled) - they need a one-on-one with you.
- Great attitude, poor ability (The Go-Getter) - they need training from you or from the Superstar.
- Poor attitude, poor ability (The Poison) - they either need time and clear guidance to modify their behavior, or they need to be removed…like, yesterday.

Decide how to prioritize your daily schedule in order to maximize effectiveness.

Tony Gambill, founder and CEO of ClearView Leadership and contributor to *Forbes Magazine* writes:

> "The most important decision a leader makes is how to invest their most valuable resources: Time and Energy. One of the biggest challenges I hear from leaders is finding enough time to focus on the most strategic parts of their roles. Too often, leaders feel overwhelmed by having to respond to the constant barrage of urgent issues that end up consuming most of their time and energy, leaving them scrambling to find "extra" time to try to achieve the most important responsibilities of their

---

[13] Kate Ashford, How To manage Toxic Employees. Monster.com. https://www.monster.com/career-advice/article/manage-a-toxic-employee

role. The dilemma often sounds like this: "I know this is important, but I am already spread too thin…"[14]

In my individual coaching sessions with leaders—as well as in my group coaching and consulting sessions—I often hear this profound sense of overwhelm. There is so much to do, and leaders often do not know where to start. There is always a mountain of paperwork and a never-ending to-do list, and a sense of dread often comes when you realize you are sitting at a table preparing to eat an elephant with just a plastic fork and a butter knife. As an emerging leader, often this anxiety is exacerbated by the realization that you are now not only responsible for prioritizing and completing the tasks of your own day, but you are also responsible for helping each of the employees you lead to do the same, every single day.

Sarah Carver describes this pain very well:

"There never seems to be enough time in the day to accomplish everything that needs to get done. With many competing demands on time, it may feel like every task is urgent. The feeling of 'putting out fires' makes it difficult to determine which tasks should be completed first and which are able to wait…Prioritizing involves identifying critical tasks and managing them without getting distracted by less important matters. In the workplace, prioritizing is the process of deciding what needs to be done, when, and by whom. Prioritizing effectively prevents the last-minute scramble as key deadlines approach."[15]

Great leaders must decide to prioritize their day to yield maximum effectiveness and minimal anxiety. I have two bits of advice for you

---

[14] Tony Gambill, Leadership Practices to Prioritize Your Time and Energy, Forbes.com. August 25, 2021. https://www.forbes.com/sites/tonygambill/2021/08/25/3-leadership-practices-to-prioritize-your-time-and-energy/?sh=2d3201d714ff

[15] Sarah Carver, *Great Leaders Prioritize. Sigma Assessment Systems.* https://www.sigmaassessmentsystems.com/prioritize/#:~:text=Prioritizing%20involves%20identifying%20critical%20tasks,scramble%20as%20key%20deadlines%20approach.

regarding this need for prioritization. The first is this: make sure your priorities align with your supervisor's priorities for you. We already discussed this idea back in Chapter 1, so I won't repeat the entire point here. Suffice it to say that my first response to leaders who ask for my help in prioritizing their day is, "Get your priorities from your supervisor, first."

My second piece of advice comes from former US President Dwight D. Eisenhower. This advice has become very popular over the years within the business world thanks to Stephen Covey discussing it in his classic work, *The 7 Habits of Highly Effective People*[16] **The Eisenhower Matrix** is as close to perfect as I have found on this subject, and, since I believe in working smarter rather than always working harder, I see no need to reinvent the wheel. Let's take a closer look.

To begin with, it is important to distinguish between *urgent* and *important* tasks. An urgent task is one that requires your immediate attention. It is something that must be done now, and it is something for which there will be serious negative consequences and repercussions if it is not done immediately. An important task is one that does not require immediate attention but is one that helps you to achieve your long-term goals. It does not have to be done right this second, and maybe not even today or this week, but they are still very important.

---

[16] Stephen Covey, The 7 Habits of Highly Effective People, 30th Anniv. Ed. (New York: Simon and Schuster, 2020).

URGENT AND IMPORTANT	URGENT BUT NOT IMPORTANT
The tasks in that first quadrant—those that are urgent and important—should be your top priority at the beginning of your day. Examples of tasks in this first quadrant are: ● Project deadlines; ● Sending product shipments on time; and/or ● Handling a client complaint;	Those tasks that are urgent but not important, the third quadrant, are candidates for delegation. But remember: only the superstars on your team are ones to whom you delegate your responsibilities. Examples include: ● Non-essential meetings; ● Some emails and interoffice communication; and/or ● Non-essential interruptions from coworkers.
NOT URGENT BUT IMPORTANT	**NEITHER URGENT NOR IMPORTANT**
Those tasks that are not urgent but are yet important, the second quadrant, should be scheduled for completion after the completion of the tasks in that first quadrant. Examples include: ● Strategic planning sessions; ● Attending professional development or training courses; and/or ● Creating a training curriculum to be used in-house.	Finally, those tasks that are neither urgent nor important, the fourth quadrant, are to be deleted. After all, they are of no importance and carry with them no urgency. Perhaps these tasks can be delegated to your interns (if you have any) or your non-Superstars. Some examples within this quadrant are: ● Surfing the web at your desk; ● Scrolling through social media posts; and/or ● Playing video games.

Since you have already seen how a matrix works in determining the four types of employees you have, we now will use our newfound matrix proficiency to help you prioritize your day. The Eisenhower Matrix also yields four distinct categories:

1. urgent and important.
2. not urgent but important.
3. urgent but not important; and
4. neither urgent nor important.

The tasks in that first quadrant—those that are urgent and important—should be your top priority at the beginning of your day. Examples of tasks in this first quadrant are:

- Project deadlines.
- Sending product shipments on time; and/or
- Handling a client complaint.

Those tasks that are not urgent but are yet important, the second quadrant, should be scheduled for completion after the completion of the tasks in that first quadrant. Examples include:

- Strategic planning sessions.
- Attending professional development or training courses; and/or
- Creating a training curriculum to be used in-house.

Those tasks that are urgent but not important, the third quadrant, are candidates for delegation. But remember: only the superstars on your team are ones to whom you delegate your responsibilities. Examples include:

- Non-essential meetings.
- Some emails and interoffice communication; and/or
- Non-essential interruptions from coworkers.

Finally, those tasks that are neither urgent nor important, the fourth quadrant, are to be deleted. They are of no importance and carry with them no urgency. These tasks can be delegated to your interns (if you have any) or your non-Superstars. Some examples within this quadrant are:

- Surfing the web at your desk.
- Scrolling through social media posts; and/or
- Playing video games.

The activities from this Fourth and final quadrant could be used to reward yourself after a long day of demanding work. However, they should not be done while you're at work, because ultimately, they are timewasters.

A final word on prioritizing your day: if you are unsure about which of your tasks may fall into which quadrant, seek out your mentor or another leader you respect and trust and ask for their input. Don't be afraid to ask for help.

Please learn this lesson sooner than I did: the leader does not have to have all the answers. In fact, I never trust a leader who never feels the need to say, "Hmmm, I don't know. That's a great question. Let's find an answer together." A great leader knows when to admit they're stuck, but also knows who they can turn to for help. Free yourself from the trap of feeling like you must always have it all together. If the person is a true mentor to you, they won't mind your leaning on them occasionally. That's the very definition of a mentor.

Decide to be the type of leader others want to follow.

I write this portion of the book as a direct response to a common question I receive, especially from emerging leaders: "What type of leader should I be?"

I am fond of saying that everyone is a teacher—they can either teach you what to do, or they can teach you what not to do—the latter, often unintentionally. Here is another homework assignment for you. Answer these two questions and provide specific examples of each:

1. Who is/was the best, most effective leader you have ever served under, observed, or read about? What qualities do you feel makes/made them the best?
2. Who is/was the worst, least effective leader you have ever served under, observed, or read about? What qualities do you feel makes/made them the worst?

Now, here is your follow-up task. Try your best to emulate those leaders you listed in response to the first question and try your best to be completely unlike those leaders you listed in response to the second question. That will get you started on your journey to answer the question, "What type of leader should I be?"

But of course, there is more. I suggest that there are four qualities that you must decide upon fostering in order to be the type of leader others want to follow. Remember, you want to be seen as the "go-to person" within your organization—perhaps, even, within your industry. You want to be the leader to whom other leaders come for advice and mentoring. You want to position yourself to be head-and-shoulders above other leaders in similar situations. Most people are satisfied with mediocrity, but you are not most people!

So, I share with you the four essential qualities, in no particular order, of followable leaders. They are:

1. proficiency.
2. integrity.
3. benevolence; and
4. humility.

1. Proficiency. Simply put, proficiency speaks to how competent you are. This seems like a no-brainer, but you might be surprised to learn how many leaders I have encountered over the years who, frankly, were not very skilled at their job. Though they may have been super nice people, these leaders were more cut out to be followers than leaders. They were timid, often afraid of making decisions because they were afraid of making mistakes. They were often emotional decision-makers and, consequently, often made the wrong decisions.

I have also encountered some leaders who simply do not know how to talk to people: they were rude, sarcastic, passive aggressive, profane, insulting, and verbal bullies. And to top it all off, they were often insecure because they had people on their teams who they knew would be much better than they were at leading the team. I once encountered a leader—a CEO, actually—who told me he had never offered training at his company before because he was worried that if he trained people, they might "become full of themselves" and their newfound knowledge and leave him for greener pastures. I immediately told him to find another consultant, because I simply refused to work with someone with that attitude. Not all money is good money.

So, are you not just good but *great* at what you do? If not, are you willing to learn and grow? Do you want the spotlight to shine only on you, or are you one who gets joy from seeing your entire team rise to superstar status? You see, the best leaders are not only those who are good as individual performers; the best leaders make everyone around them better as well. The best leaders do not simply develop themselves; they develop those around them. If your employees are not better performers and better human beings by having been exposed to you, you are failing them and you are failing yourself.

2. Integrity. A common definition of integrity is the quality of being honest and having strong moral principles. Are you honest in your words and in your dealings with others? When your employees hear you make a promise, can they count on you to fulfill it? Do you treat everyone with the same degree of respect and professionalism, or does someone have to believe like you, look like you, live where you live, vote how you vote, worship how you worship (if they even worship at all), etc., for you to treat them well? Can your employees share sensitive, personal information with you and fully expect that you will not broadcast it in the company newsletter? I'll come back to this definition of integrity in a moment, but first let me share with you my own personal view on this subject.

My own definition of integrity is *a strict adherence to one's own code of conduct or values.* In other words, to be a person of integrity means to know what one's own values are and to refuse to violate them. An ancient philosopher even defined integrity as who you are when nobody is watching you. I do what I do not because I have an audience but because what I do is an outgrowth of who I am.

I'll share a personal example with you. Some years ago – in my late 20s - I was presented with a business offer that would have earned me a high six figures. It was a corporate sponsorship that would have allowed me to travel the globe speaking and presenting. A colleague of mine whom I met while we were both members of the National Speakers Association had a similar corporate sponsorship and recommended me to this company. However, the corporation that was making the offer was one of the largest, most profitable breweries in the United States. I turned the offer down, because I don't drink alcohol (in fact I never have) and I have family members who have struggled with substance abuse over the years. I have buried friends who died of alcoholism and other types of substance abuse.

For me, the choice I had to make was clear, but clear does not mean easy. A high six-figure deal in my 20s would have been quite a boon to me, but I honestly would never have felt good about my associating with a brewery. Of course, I'm not saying that's the decision everyone should make, but it was my decision and I still do not regret it.

You must decide what your own lines-in-the-sand will be, and you must be willing to sacrifice some of the material trappings you might desire in order to hold on to your integrity. At the end of the day, you must live with yourself. Can you live with yourself while working for an organization that violates your own moral code, whatever that code may be? I have a friend who turned down an offer to become the human resources director of a large casino because she doesn't believe in gambling. I have another friend who left a high paying job after the CEO made some anti-LGBTQ comments and used a demeaning slur toward that community in a very public forum. Yet another friend refused a significant job offer because the organization had a record of paying female executives much less than what they paid their male counterparts. I can't tell you exactly what your code should be. I will simply tell you that you should know what it is and be willing to stand for it, regardless of what the cost might be to you. It's okay if we disagree with one another on this point, but that's my story and I'm sticking to it.

Speaking of that first definition of integrity - displaying honesty in your dealings with your employees - I recently conducted a company-wide training for an organization in the southern region of the United States. I was there to help them work through what the organizers of the event referred to as a "highly toxic work environment filled with distrust and dissatisfaction." I wasn't rattled; I've dealt with similar scenarios many times before. I jumped in with my typical discussion starters so I could build rapport and learn what the company looked like from the employees' point of view...and noticed something unsettling: the employees would not speak freely and openly when their supervisors were in the room. In fact, before anyone would even attempt to answer a question, they would make eye contact with their supervisor first, and then they would look back at me, emotionless.

Well, anybody who knows me knows that one of my mantras is, "When in charge, take charge." I asked the supervisors to excuse themselves from the proceedings, and I very directly said to those employees remaining in the room, "Okay, gang. Tell me why you all seem so apprehensive to share when your supervisors are in the room."

"Dr. Noble," many of the 50 attendees began, "if we say anything the supervisors do not like, they will retaliate against us after you leave. They've done it before. We've learned to just keep our mouths shut."

I then answered, "If I promise not to give any of your names, do you mind if I share your feelings with your supervisors?" They agreed, and after the training was complete, I made my report to the supervisors, along with my recommendations for how to remedy the situation. Months later, in a follow-up visit, the employees themselves told me that they noticed a change in the attitude of management, and they even told me that the most egregious "retaliator" had since been removed from the company. That company still has more progress to make, but I am immensely proud of them for having taken those crucial initial steps.

To be a person of integrity, you must know what you believe in, and foster an atmosphere of trust. You must have a clear, consistent idea of right and wrong. One of my graduate school professors, Dr. John Diamond, once said on the concept of morality, "If what I do or how I act does not come from a place of genuine concern for you to live your best, happiest, most fulfilled life, then it is morally wrong, and I must discard it." [17]While we may not all agree upon an exact definition of "right" and "wrong," I believe we all can sense when a leader lacks the type of integrity that makes them someone we wish to follow. That leads to our next quality of followable leaders:

3. Benevolence. Are you the type of leader who genuinely cares about the people you lead? Do you view them as partners, or do you view them as objects whose sole purpose is to help you achieve your personal career goals? How kind are you? How friendly are you? Do you know their names? Do you know anything about their families? While we cannot be expected to treat them as if we are the psychologists and they are our patients, are we at least concerned about what may be troubling them beyond the walls of the office?

My school principal Lionel Ward taught me this by example when I was about 11 years old, when he asked me—as president of the student council—to join him in escorting the Little Rock School District Superintendent Dr. Paul Masem on a tour of the building at Rightsell Intermediate School. As the three of us were walking down one of the hallways, Mr. Ward said, "Excuse me one moment," and interrupted Dr. Masem mid-sentence to stop and speak to the school building custodian, Mr. Richie. I immediately thought to myself,

---

[17] John Diamond, "THE 600 : Introduction to Theology and Philosophy" (lecture, Interdenominational Theological Center, Atlanta, GA, November 19, 1996).

"Uh oh, Mr. Ward just interrupted his boss. He's going to be in trouble, I bet."

Mr. Ward stood face-to-face with Mr. Richie, greeted him with a warm smile, and started a conversation with him by asking about his daughter, who had recently been sick. After listening to Mr. Richie's medical report about his daughter, my principal then said, "Please tell her that Mr. Ward says hello and wishes her a speedy recovery. You have my home number, so call me if you all need anything." All the while, Dr. Masem stood patiently and silently with a smile on his face, and then looked down at me and nodded his head, as if to say, "Now *that's* how we are supposed to treat people." Mr. Ward then rejoined the tour and said, "So Dr. Masem, you were saying?"

I have never forgotten that lesson, even though at the time I didn't even know the definition of the word "benevolence." As the age-old adage goes, "People don't care how much you know until they know how much you care."

4. Humility. Whenever I think of the word humility, I remember a scene from the 90s television show *Martin,* starring Martin Lawrence. Lawrence was known for playing various characters on his show, one of whom was a martial arts instructor named Dragonfly Jones. At the start of a martial arts class, he introduced himself to the students by saying, "Hello everybody. I'm Dragonfly Jones, and it's a pleasure for you to meet me."

Dragonfly Jones is one of my all-time favorite sitcom characters, but it would be scary for a leader to have that mindset. I have seen far too many leaders who honestly believe that their employees should be filled with awe and wonder at the prospect of working under such an amazing specimen of leadership. I like to look at it the other way around: as a leader, I am the one who is privileged to come beside you and help lift you to a place of excellence. My good friend Darius Clayton, a great young leader in his own right, defines leadership with one word: service. I think we would all do well to adopt that definition for ourselves.

The best leaders are not those who seek to improve their lot and their lot alone; the best leaders are those who realize that it takes a team to accomplish the goals of organizations. It was your outstanding performance as an individual that brought your name to the forefront of the promotion list to begin with, but now, it is no longer simply about you—it's about the whole team. That type of leadership requires a good, strong dose of humility.

Unfortunately, we live in a world that often equates humility with weakness, so it takes a lot of fortitude to set one's ego aside and propel a team to higher heights. It is worth doing, however, as humble leaders are considered more approachable, more forgiving of mistakes, and more willing to acknowledge others for jobs well done. This, in turn, can motivate employees to become more creative and to work harder. Humility becomes even more important as a leader's responsibility increases, because with greater responsibility comes the opportunity for greater success—which, unfortunately, can be accompanied by greater arrogance and self-promotion on the part of the leader if you're not careful.[18]

Admitting Mistakes and Apologizing Effectively

I conclude this chapter and this point with another aspect of humility: the ability to admit one's mistakes and make amends. I hate to be the one to break it to you, but there is no such thing as leadership without mistakes. Those who are perfectionists often have an exceedingly tough time in leadership because they beat themselves up whenever they fall. While a hallmark of being a strong leader is in making wise decisions, there will be times when—no matter how

---

[18] Charlotte Stith-Flood, *It's Not Hard To Be Humble: The Role of Humility in Leadership.* American Academy of Family Physicians. June 2018. https://www.aafp.org/pubs/fpm/issues/2018/0500/p25.html#:~:text=Humility%20is%20an%20important%20but,as%20a%20leader's%20responsibility%20increases.

careful you are—you will foul up, fall flat on your face, let yourself down, let your team down, or even let your whole organization down. Mistakes are inevitable.

May I share a secret with you? People will be a whole lot more forgiving of you when you do mess up if you handle it correctly.

So, how should we handle our mistakes in leadership? Here are my suggestions:

1. Apologize without making excuses or using the word "but." Mistakes are not what bother people. What bothers people is when you make a mistake and either refuse to admit it, or you admit it but make excuses about it. The following are NOT acceptable apologies:

- *"I apologize for _____; but the reason why I did it is _____."*

This makes an excuse for your behavior, completely nullifying your apology. There are distinct differences between explanations and excuses. The purpose of an explanation is to present facts and discuss the cause of an action or an event. The purpose of an excuse is to make oneself appear faultless and to assign blame elsewhere. If explaining the reason behind your action is meant to clear up a misunderstanding, then it may be appropriate. However, if your purpose is simply to absolve yourself of any culpability, then you've drifted into excuses rather than explanations.

"I'm so sorry you feel that way."

This blames people for their own feelings or for their reaction to our actions/words towards them. This is commonly referred to as *gaslighting*. Redirecting the narrative so that the other person is at fault when the fault actually lies with you is emotional manipulation, and it can be very destructive. The person who has been on the receiving end of the unacceptable behavior begins to question themselves, even questioning their own recollection of what happened.

"Nobody's perfect."

This is defensive and deflective, and neither response is acceptable. Apologies such as this one are often "an attempt to rebuild or strengthen your 'I am a good person' narrative because the apology seemingly is offering care for the other person…Care is about supporting another person, not about protecting oneself."[19]

"Well, what about that time when you did _____?"

This is a textbook definition of deflection and is unacceptable. Apologies should be focused on our own mistakes and actions rather than on the other person's reaction to our mistakes and actions. When an apology focuses more on the offended person's response than our own acts, it becomes a toxic apology and reeks of insincerity.

Instead of these passive-aggressive apologies, try simply saying something like:

"I am terribly sorry about (or I apologize for) this. How can I make this right, and ensure it never happens again?"

Mistakes are inevitable in leadership. It is how you handle the mistakes you make that will make or break you.

2. Re-evaluate your leadership style. A mistake is an opportunity for you to do some self-reflection—ask yourself, "Is my approach to leadership what is causing me to make these mistakes?" If you're not sure, you may want to ask these questions of yourself:

- Are my mistakes the result of my making decisions too quickly without careful analysis first?

---

[19] Kathleen Rea, *"I'm sorry my actions triggered you": Apologies that deflect responsibility.* October 30, 2021. https://contactimprovconsentculture. com/2021/10/30/im-sorry-my-actions-triggered-you-apologies-that-deflect-responsibility-and-can-set-the-stage-for-abusive-behaviors/

- Am I making mistakes because I am not consulting a mentor who may be a bit more experienced and wiser than I?
- Are my mistakes the result of an over-inflated ego?
- Do I genuinely value the opinions of the people I lead, or do I view myself as the resident expert?
- Am I allowing any personal dislikes or biases to affect my judgment?
- Am I assuming everyone knows what my expectations are rather than clearly explaining what they are?

3. **Once you have re-evaluated your leadership style, make the necessary adjustments, apologize to those who have been affected, and refuse to beat yourself up about it.** The best apology is changed behavior. Once you have answered the tough questions, make the necessary corrections. If you're not sure how to change, speak with a mentor whose opinion you respect or speak with those whom you lead and ask them, "How can I be a better leader for you?" Seek out information on how to make significant changes in your leadership style. That information can come from books, articles, periodicals, or even your therapist. Fix what is broken. Change what is ineffective. Do what needs to be done or stop doing what does not need to be done. You have already made the necessary apologies, now change your behavior to reflect your sincerity. You will notice that your transparency and vulnerability as a leader will set an example for your team and even open the door for them to follow suit.

I recently led a two-day leadership retreat for a long-standing client of mine, a major nonprofit organization in the southern US with an operating budget of $20 million dollars. At the conclusion of the first day of the retreat, which was spent exclusively with the 10-person executive leadership team, I said, "Okay, we have discussed some of your triumphs over this past year, as well as some of your mistakes. Tomorrow, when your employees and direct reports join us for Day Two, I want each of you, one by one, to stand up and apologize to your people for the mistakes you have made, and pledge to do better." Each one of them agreed, though two of them were less than enthusiastic about the prospect.

The next day, at the conclusion of the apologies (a couple of which were tearful, and all of which were quite sincere), the ballroom of that hotel was filled with crying employees, many of whom had never had a supervisor or manager ever apologize to them for anything. But that's not the end of the story—many of the employees themselves then followed the lead of the executive team and started publicly apologizing for some of their behaviors. Some employees apologized for spreading gossip; some employees apologized for being chronic complainers; some employees apologized for failing to be consistent in their communication; one employee even apologized for her own toxic behavior toward her colleagues (her words—not mine).

Only once did I have to redirect one of the employees who began her apology with the words, "Well, I don't think I'm as bad as everybody else always says I am, but I want to apologize anyway." I calmly but firmly responded and said, "Try that apology again. This time don't excuse your behavior or your colleagues' perceptions. Simply apologize." She acknowledged her error and restated her apology this way: "I have created some tension in my department with my actions, my attitude, and my words; and for that, I am truly, truly sorry."

At the conclusion of what was quite an emotional day, I told them what I now tell you: "The apologies have been offered and accepted. I need you now to pledge to not bring them up again, and to allow everyone, including yourself, to start over with a clean slate. Leave these issues buried. It's time for a new life." Many of the attendees told me at the end of the day that it had been the best day they had ever spent as employees of the company.

Several months after the leadership retreat, the CEO informed me that one of the leaders who had previously come under fire for their overly aggressive attitude and had made one of the tearful apologies that day had to place one of his employees on administrative leave. The employee remarked to the CEO, "Months ago, he would have handled that in a totally different way. But today, he was clear and assertive without being nasty or mean. I couldn't even be angry. I deserved the disciplinary action, and he handled it more professionally than I thought he would. He is really growing in his leadership."

Wrap-up

Now let's review. In this chapter, you have learned:

- Three major truths about decision making.
- How to get crystal clear about the direction into which you need to lead your team.
- Why helping your team clearly understand the bigger purpose of the work they do is the single most important key to motivating them.
- How to determine what each of your employees needs from you for them to become Superstars.
- How to utilize The Eisenhower Matrix to help you prioritize and maximize your effectiveness; and
- The right and wrong ways to apologize when you've made a mistake.

Focusing upon the right decisions to make as an emerging leader will go a long way toward getting you off to a strong start and will help you to reduce your stress levels in the long term. The inverse is true as well: the less stressed you are, the better your ability to stay focused will be. Also, keep in mind that laser focus and reduced stress will help you make an impact much more quickly and will create shortcuts to effectiveness. Stress is one of the biggest hurdles a leader must overcome, and the next chapter is designed to help you do just that.

Chapter 2 Implementation Tasks:

1. Answer the Three Navigational Questions for yourself:

    -   *"What is my purpose as the leader of my team/this organization?"*
    -   *"What is the purpose of this department/team/group that I'm leading?"*
    -   *"What is the purpose of this organization as a whole?"*

2. Answer those same Three Navigational Questions for each of the people you lead, changing the wording for the first question to "What is my purpose as the _____ on this team?" Fill in the blank with whatever their title or position may be. The only answer that should differ from person to person will be the answer to that first question.

3. Inform your team members, individually and as a group, what the higher or deeper purpose of their job is.

4. Get out of your office and get to know each of your employees individually, using some of the suggestions made in this chapter.

5. Determine what each employee needs most from you by categorizing them according to the Four-Quality Matrix (The Superstar, The Disgruntled, The Go-Getter, or The Poison).

6. Print a copy of The Eisenhower Matrix (or draw up your own) and begin to use it daily as a prioritizer until you get the hang of it.

7. Answer the questions: **A)** Who is/was the best, most effective leader you have ever served under, observed, or read about? What qualities do you feel makes/made them the best? **B)** Who is/was the worst, least effective leader you have ever served under, observed, or read about? What qualities do you feel makes/made them the worst?

8. Evaluate yourself according to the 4 Essential Qualities of Follow-able Leaders. Which ones are you already good at? Which ones do you need to improve upon? If you're not

sure you can be objective, ask someone who knows you and whose opinion you trust to evaluate you.

Chapter 2 Reactions:

1. What did I already know?

2. Of what was I reminded? How will I act upon those reminders?

3. What was brand new information to me?

Handling the Stress
of Leadership

It shocked me, because it had never happened before: my scores of friends were not there for me. I had asked for help, and they had not shown up for me as they had always done in the past. I was confused, alone, and—I must admit—bordering upon angry.

I have some incredibly good friends; many of them have been in my life since our childhood days in Little Rock. We often keep up with each other, we post silly jokes, funny memes, and inspirational quotes to each other, we celebrate one another's family milestones. Above all, we always offer advice to one another. There have been many times when I have needed suggestions, guidance, and help with my research projects, and my friends have always shown up, sent detailed responses, and have even followed up on the phone with me if they felt I needed it.

But not this time. This time, my many friends fell silent. Only ten of them mustered responses when I asked my friends on social media:

"What do you do to reduce stress and anxiety as a leader?"

Each comment gave me a response like this one:

"Derrick, I don't know how to handle stress at all. In fact, I was following the post to read the answers, because I don't have an answer—and I need one."

I decided I would begin reaching out to the hundreds of friends I hadn't heard from, many of whom liked the post on various social media platforms but failed to respond. After speaking with the 25th person on my friends list, I decided to stop reaching out altogether, because a clear pattern had emerged: they had each given me the same answer.

Stress can wreak havoc on one's mind and body. The American Psychological Association Dictionary of Psychology defines stress as the physiological and/or psychological response to internal or external factors, which can cause a state of strain or tension, and can directly influence how one feels and behaves.[20] Stress can emanate from many sources, but one of the major sources of stress is the workplace. An elevated level of workplace stress can then go on to affect one's happiness, productivity, relationships, and tenure at an organization, which can then lead to high employee turnover, low productivity, and a pervading sense of unhappiness.[21]

Colonial Life and Accident Insurance Company joined forces with Dynata, the world's largest first-party data platform, to conduct a survey of 1,505 full-time U.S. employees between the ages of 18 and 70 about workplace stress. Some of the findings of that study are as follows:

- More than 20 percent of workers spend more than five hours at work each week thinking about the very factors that create their stress.
- Seventy percent of workers admitted to losing between one to five hours of work per week to handling (or mishandling) stress.
- Forty-one percent of employees surveyed said workplace stress made them less productive.

---

[20] https://dictionary.apa.org/stress
[21] https://www.myshortlister.com/insights/workplace-stress-statistics

- Fifteen percent admitted they were, at the time of the survey, actively seeking out new, less stressful employment; and
- Fourteen percent said that stress made them miss work more frequently than normal.[22]

Research conducted by Caitlin Mazur in early 2022 for Zippia reveals even more staggering statistics about workplace stress:

- Seventy-six percent of US workers report that workplace stress affects their personal relationships.
- Depression-induced absenteeism costs US businesses $51 billion a year, as well as an additional $26 billion in treatment costs.
- More than 50 percent of workers are not engaged at work because of stress, leading to a loss of productivity.
- Sixty-three percent of US workers are ready to quit their jobs due to stress, and 16 percent of workers have already quit a past job due to stress.
- Only 40 percent of employees who suffer from stress have talked to their employer about it. In addition, 34 percent of workers don't feel safe reporting stress because they think it would be interpreted as a lack of interest or unwillingness to do the activity; and
- Work-related stress causes 120,000 deaths and results in $190 billion in healthcare costs yearly.[23]

Are you convinced, yet, of the potentially destructive power of stress? If not, let's take a closer look at Zippia's research and see the effects stress can have upon one's body.

---

[22] https://www.coloniallife.com/about/newsroom/2019/march/stressed-workers-costing-employers-billions

[23] Caitlin Mazur, 40+ Worrisome Workplace Stress Statistics [2022]: Facts, Causes, and Trends. Zippia. January 23, 2022. https://www.zippia.com/advice/workplace-stress-statistics/

The Physiological Effects of Stress

- Stress caused sleep deprivation for 66 percent of employees in 2018.
- More than half of those who responded to the Zippia survey questions confessed that they often have 12-hour workdays. They also admitted to frequently skipping lunch because of job stress and demands. Sixty-two percent of workers said they leave work with neck pain, 44 percent reported stressed-out eyes, and 34 percent reported having trouble sleeping. This type of ongoing stress can have colossally negative effects upon one's physical and mental health.
- 120,000 deaths are a direct result of excessive workplace stress, resulting in nearly $190 billion in health care costs each year.
- Workplace-induced depression leads to $51 billion in costs due to absenteeism and $26 billion in treatment costs. Workers who are frequently stressed incur healthcare costs twice as high as other employees.[24]

But while stress can clearly be destructive for the employee, the effects of stress upon leadership can be even higher.

The Double-Sided Pressures of Leadership

There is a type of stress often experienced by leaders that their employees may not ever experience. I refer to it as double-sided pressure. First, there is:

---

[24] Caitlin Mazur, 40+ Worrisome Workplace Stress Statistics [2022]: Facts, Causes, and Trends. Zippia. January 23, 2022. https://www.zippia.com/advice/workplace-stress-statistics/

1. Pressure from the top. Your direct supervisor, or the board of directors, or whoever provides oversight for you is pressuring you to produce results in your new role as leader. As we discussed in previous chapters, emerging leaders often do not have the luxury of moving slowly and deliberately. You were hired because the organization needs results, and they would much rather see them sooner than later. That type of pressure can be a stressor; because it creates internal questions with which emerging leaders often wrestle, including:

- If I fail to produce positive results quickly, how long will I be able to keep this job?
- How embarrassed will I be if I get demoted or even terminated because of my failure to produce?
- What types of trouble will a lack of income produce for me and/or my family?

While all employees can indeed experience that type of top-down pressure, there is another layer of added pressure for leaders, and that is:

2. Pressure from below. To use a sports analogy, all players want to be a part of a winning team, which means having a coach who knows how to guide them to success. A good athlete needs a coach who will push them farther than they have ever been pushed. At the same time, no athlete wants to be pushed so hard that it makes them want to quit the team. Your employees will often have this mindset relative to you and your style of leadership. They will think the following:

- Push me, but not too hard.
- Be hard on me, but don't be a jerk.
- Expect more from me, but hey—let's not be unrealistic, here.
- Tell me how to improve but praise me when I'm doing well. In fact, praise me publicly; coach me privately.

- I'm okay with your yelling at my slacker teammates, but never—and I mean *never*—do that to me, even when I'm the one slacking.

As the leader, you feel the stress of having to balance being the type of coach who wins championships with being the type of coach who doesn't make your players want to choke you during practice! (Do the names Latrell Sprewell and P.J. Carlesimo ring any bells?)[25]

In addition to this double-sided pressure, there are two other major stressors for the emerging leader:

3. Imposter syndrome. According to the American Psychological Association, psychologists Suzanne Imes, PhD, and Pauline Rose Clance, PhD, first described imposter syndrome in the 1970s. ("Staying Grounded, Finding Support is Essential to Combating Imposter ...") This phenomenon often occurs among high achievers who, for whatever reason, doubt whether they are worthy of the success they have achieved. They often attribute their accomplishments to luck or to having been in the right place at the right time.

Most of all, those who wrestle with imposter syndrome are afraid that others will eventually realize that they are not as talented as they seem. They worry their colleagues will one day realize that they are unworthy of the leadership position they currently hold. I believe that any leader who has accomplished anything of significance has doubted themselves at least once, and asked, "Do I really deserve to be here? Can I really handle this position? How long will it be before I fall flat on my face?"

And if imposter syndrome and double-sided pressure were not enough, there is a fourth major stressor leaders experience:

---

[25] On December 1, 1997, Latrell Sprewell—a member of the Golden State Warriors of the NBA—famously threatened to kill his coach, PJ Carlesimo, during practice one day when the coach instructed Sprewell to put more energy into his passing. Sprewell then wrestled Coach Carlesimo to the ground and choked him. Sprewell was suspended and was eventually traded to another team.

4. The pressure to not lose oneself amid leadership. Is it possible to be an effective leader and still have a satisfying, fulfilling life outside of the job? For many leaders, the answer is no—but that's the wrong answer.

I know far too many leaders who wear their overwork as a badge of honor. That mantra of "first one in the office, last one to leave" is an extremely unhealthy way to function. I'm fond of telling my executive coaching clients to be deliberate about reframing negative experiences and turning them into positives. One of the positive aspects of the worldwide COVID-19 pandemic was that, in 2020, the workforce began to realize that people could be just as productive from home as they could be in the office. It no longer makes you a hero to spend your life in the office, giving yourself for a job that would move on almost immediately if you were to die from a workplace stress-induced stroke or heart attack.

I don't mean to be morbid, but I want you to learn this lesson sooner than I did. I lay on my back in my doctor's office in my early 30s while leading a nonprofit organization, and my doctor told me, "You have to be one of the unhealthiest young men I've ever seen. Either you learn better ways of handling the pressures of your job, or you will be dead in six months. And I'm sorry, but *if* I were to attend the funeral, it would only be to tell the gathered congregation, 'He was my patient, and I warn you: don't be like this guy.'"

Ouch.

Those words stung, but not as badly as the chest pains, headaches, and restricted blood flow that had led me to the doctor's office in the first place. That reality check started me on a path that continues to this day. I have learned to handle stress before it handles me, and I'll share below some ways I have learned to have a life aside from my work. Following that, I will allow space for my friends, each strong leaders with years of experience and success under their belts, to share with you their own ways. They have some highly creative suggestions for dealing with the stresses that accompany leadership. Please pay close attention to the following advice for leaders, from leaders.

Tips For Successfully Handling Stress

Far too many leaders handle stress in some destructive ways—they either overeat or they starve themselves; they drink caffeine in unhealthy doses; they turn to alcohol or drugs (both prescription and illegal); and so on. While I have never taken the alcohol or drug route—I've never even tried them, nor have I ever wanted to - my vice was sugar. A bag of chocolate chip cookies would be a meal to me, topped off with a bowl or two of sugary breakfast cereal. Just *having* stress can negatively affect you. Stress can cause hair loss, heart disease, suppress your immune system, and even accelerate the aging process. I first want to share with you my personal tips (which I have learned from mentors—or, often, the hard way) for handling the inevitable stress that accompanies leadership positions. I have practiced these all for many years because they work wonderfully well for me.

1. See a licensed therapist. We have to remove the stigma that sitting down to talk to a counselor or therapist means you're "crazy." (As a matter of fact, I hate that word.) There is absolutely nothing crazy about sitting down with a professional to help you sort through situations in your life that may be difficult for you to handle on your own. Every leader needs to have regular conversations with a licensed therapist who is skilled at helping you unpack stress. Simply acknowledging that you are feeling stressed is the first step, but it is certainly not the only step. You then need to understand the reasons why particular situations are stressors for you.

For example, I felt stressed out, unhappy, and physically ill on my first job after having graduated with my master's degree. When I sat down with a therapist—the first time I had done so since my freshman year of college eight years earlier—she helped me to realize that the reason why I was so unhappy and stressed was because my supervisor was treating me the same way I was often treated during childhood: I was berated, cursed at, belittled, and insulted. I was a grown man feeling like that same scared child trembling with fear that he might be cursed at, bullied, belittled, or even hit with an open-handed slap (which happened more often during my childhood than I care to remember). My workplace gave me stress because it transported me back to a most unhappy period of my childhood.

Once you figure out the reasons behind your stress, you can handle your stress in healthy ways. I repeat: see a therapist, even if you're not feeling stressed out. The benefits of talking to a professional on a regular basis far outweigh any potential embarrassment you think it may bring.

If you're one of those people who believe the only person you should talk to is a spiritual guide, then by all means, see your pastor or your priest. However, I still strongly recommend that you sit down with a licensed therapist. Though your spiritual leader may be well intentioned, if they do not have extensive training in counseling techniques, it may not be extremely helpful. I consider myself a spiritual man, but "pray it away" is not always the best advice, and certainly shouldn't be the *only* advice. That's one man's opinion; feel free to disagree. But let's agree upon this, at least: go sit down and talk to *someone*, now.

2. Find or rediscover a hobby and regularly enjoy it. What do you enjoy doing for relaxation? Do you like to go fishing? Do you like to cook? Do you enjoy bowling? How about sewing or knitting? Do you enjoy curling up in front of the TV? How about a big bowl of popcorn to go along with that movie? Perhaps you enjoy reading or writing. Whatever it is, find it or rediscover it and start doing it on a regular basis. It doesn't matter what your hobby is, if you enjoy it, and it makes you happy or brings you peace.

Maybe you're like me, and you enjoy music, especially live music venues. I have been a huge fan of jazz since I was a fourth grader, and my oldest brother Willie played a recording for me of the jazz-fusion group Weather Report. My jazz exposure soon expanded to Miles Davis, John Coltrane, Herbie Hancock, Freddie Hubbard, Ella Fitzgerald, Louis Armstrong, Dizzy Gillespie, Art Tatum—the list goes on and on and on. I took up playing both the baritone horn and the valve trombone in concert band, marching band, and jazz band throughout my school years. I even used to sneak into jazz clubs as a teenager with my high school buddy Tony Baker, who is now Professor of Trombone at The University of North Texas. I still frequent jazz venues now, and I don't have to sneak in.

Naturally, I listen to and perform jazz as my stress reliever. Music calms me and excites me at the same time, and when I'm involved with it, I couldn't be happier! Find your hobby and enjoy it. You deserve it.

A large corporation once hired me to conduct a series of one-on-one coaching sessions with one of its mid-level managers. She was a leader whose immediate supervisor had described her as timid and submissive; she concurred with her supervisor's description of herself. Near the midway point of our eight-session series, she told me how the stress of her job coupled with the stress of parenting teenagers was almost too much for her. She lamented that she never had time for herself. I gave her an assignment to be completed immediately: "List for me five activities you enjoy doing that you haven't been able to do in a while." After she did so, I then asked her to rank those activities according to which were her favorites. Then, I gave her the next step, which leads to my third tip for handling stress:

3. Schedule down time just like you schedule your business tasks. Once that mid-level manager ranked her list of five hobbies she enjoyed but hadn't engaged in for years, I said, "Take out your calendar, and let's schedule some dates and times to enjoy these activities on your calendar."

Startled, she asked, "Um, you mean right now?"

"Yes, right now; because just like you schedule board meetings, staff meetings with your direct reports, and volleyball/soccer/basketball trips for your kids, you also need to schedule time for your hobbies. Then, what you're going to do is share this calendar with family and coworkers and tell them, 'If any of you need me on these days at these times, I will be unavailable.'"

You must make down-time and hobby time a priority for yourself. Plus, you must be willing to be held accountable for keeping those appointments, which is why I told that manager to share her new calendar with everyone in her circle.

Of course, there came the inevitable question: "But what if somebody needs me on one of these dates?"

That's a fair question, and here's my answer. You must determine if canceling your plans will be a one-time exception, or if it will become the norm because you are so needed by so many. Many people cannot make a one-time cancellation without it becoming a habit of putting everyone else's needs above their own. My thoughts on the subject are a bit cut and dry - too cut and dry for some people - but nonetheless here they are: an emergency means someone is bleeding or dying. If neither condition is present, then the issue may in fact be urgent, but it isn't an emergency. I suggest only making the exception in case of an emergency. If you don't draw the line somewhere, then you may never draw the line. If you do not take care of yourself, you may not ever be able to adequately care for others.

For example, have you ever been on an airplane and heard a flight attendant say during the safety demonstration, "If we experience a change in cabin pressure, oxygen masks will drop down from overhead. If you're traveling with a child, please put your mask on first, and then assist your child." To a parent, those instructions may sound selfish, but they tell you that because they understand that you will be better able to help your child if you are in the best position to do so. If you're struggling for oxygen, you will struggle trying to help your child, and you might both end up without oxygen because of it.

Get the picture? You have to take care of yourself if you are going to take care of those who need you, whether they are your employees or your family members. Taking care of yourself is not selfish; in fact, it is the exact opposite. Because you care about those who follow your leadership, you have to be in a position of strength so you can best be of service to them.

4. Make some type of physical activity a part of your daily routine.
We all know we need to do this; even those who hate exercise and physical activity know it's necessary. Exercise improves your overall health and even helps to improve your sense of well-being. However, many people avoid exercise because they have been incorrectly informed that they need to run a marathon or become a triathlete for exercise to be beneficial. That simply is not true. Experts within the medical community agree that any form of exercise, from aerobics to yoga, can help to relieve stress.

For example, it may help you if you change the way you approach exercise. A friend of mine once told me what really helped her was realizing she didn't have to do a bunch of boring exercises like walking on a treadmill or using an exercise bike in the typical gym. Instead, she could get a workout at a rock-climbing gym, or kayaking, or rollerblading, or skateboarding, etc. The "fun" aspect was what finally made her start getting in shape. There are many ways to get exercise that do not involve weights or gigantic rubber bands. The point is that exercise of any kind can go a long way towards helping to reduce your stress levels.

The Mayo Clinic informs us that there are four major ways in which exercise helps to relieve stress:

a) Exercise increases endorphins, which are hormones secreted within the brain whenever the body feels pain or stress. In other words, you already have naturally occurring stress-fighting material within your body, and exercise releases them.

b) Exercise reduces the negative effects of stress, including boosting your cardiovascular, digestive, and immune systems.

c) Exercise is akin to meditation; it results in more optimism, more energy, and greater focus.

d) Exercise helps improve your mood. It increases self-confidence, especially once you look in the mirror or step on the scale and see the results of your hard work.

It helps you relax and can even lower symptoms of mild depression and anxiety.[26]

Aerobic exercise, also known as cardio exercise, is any activity that raises your heart rate into that zone where the most calories and fat are burned. Harvard Medical School tells us:

"Indeed, the first steps are the hardest, and in the beginning, exercise will be more work than fun. But as you get into shape, you'll begin to tolerate exercise, then enjoy it, and finally depend on it. Regular aerobic exercise[27] will bring remarkable changes to your body, your metabolism, your heart, and your spirits."[28]

My brother Jerry, a personal trainer and former competitive bodybuilder, says that most people make exercising too complicated. Here is his advice concerning workouts:

"Depending upon how you decide to target body parts, [one should aim for] three or four days a week at no more than 45 minutes per workout. For example: let's say you choose to do full-body workouts. The daily split would look something like this:

Monday – 40 minutes
Wednesday – 30 minutes (moving faster with less rest
    between exercises)
Friday – 40 minutes.

The next week:
Monday -30 minutes
Wednesday – 40 minutes
Friday – 30 minutes

---

[26] https://www.mayoclinic.org/healthy-lifestyle/stress-management/in-depth/exercise-and-stress/art-20044469#:~:text=Examples%20include%20walking%2C%20stair%20climbing,Pencil%20it%20in.

[27] Aerobic exercise, also known as cardio exercise, is any activity that raises your heart rate into that zone where the most calories and fat are burned.

[28] https://www.health.harvard.edu/staying-healthy/exercising-to-relax

Note: The above does not include the time spent doing cardio workouts or warm-ups. If you do cardio on a lifting day, I would recommend no more than 20 minutes. If you do [cardio] on a non-lifting day, [aim for] 30 to 40 minutes.

I also think that every three months you should take at least 10 days (but no more than 14 days) off from exercise. I think people make working out too hard on their minds and bodies."[29]

My own exercise routine consists of at least 40 minutes of diverse types of cardio, five days per week. My three go-to cardio choices are the elliptical machine, boxing, and brisk walking. I try my best to do these early in the morning - like 6:00 a.m. - because I know that once my day gets started, I will become less and less likely to get my workout clothes on and make it happen. However, I really love walking in the evening, just before sunset. I will walk anywhere from 40 minutes up to 90 minutes in the evening. I find it to be a very relaxing way to end my day.

In addition to my aerobic exercise, I do strength training four or five days per week. I enjoy using the nautilus machines much more than I enjoy using free weights, for some reason. And I am always sure to have my noise-canceling headphones, blasting some mid-tempo or fast jazz (I love jazz ballads, but they make me sleepy) or some old-school R&B music, especially Stevie Wonder, The Spinners and The O'Jays.

5. Find some non-workplace friends to hang out with occasionally.
Every now and then, you need to spend time with people who are not workplace colleagues and whose presence will not make you think about work-related issues when your mind should be elsewhere. I'm not suggesting that you should not befriend your coworkers or spend time with them away from the job, but it is difficult to be around

---

[29] This entire quote is from a series of emails between Jerry and me on June 6, 2022, as I asked his advice on which equipment I should buy for my new home gym.

workplace colleagues without being tempted to discuss workplace issues.

You need a place and space where your work life does not even enter the conversation. If you do spend time with workplace colleagues away from the office, after hours, or on weekends, I strongly recommend that all of you make a pact with one another to not discuss anything about your job. That's difficult, but it may be doable. You must have a clear line of demarcation that says, "Work is work, but home is home, and as much as I can, I need to strive to keep the two separate."

Those are just some of my suggestions for how to successfully handle the stress that almost inevitably accompanies any leadership position, but especially for emerging leaders. At this point, I want to allow ten of my friends to share with you some insights into how they deal with stress. As I mentioned earlier, each of them is a leader within the world of business or education, and they are all excited to share the following tips with you.

- **Herman Botley**: Fitness Instructor and Personal Trainer – The Camp

    Transformation Center (Arlington, TX) – "Music, meditation and prayer is the perfect Rx for me to de-stress. Like you [Derrick], there's always a song in my heart and a soundtrack playing in my head 24/7."

- **Darius Clayton**: Assistant Director – Rouse's Market (Lake Charles, LA) – "I work out regularly. The results I receive help me to focus on the fact that there are rewards after the sacrifice. Also, I like to reflect on all the other accomplishments I've achieved in the past. They remind me of the times I had to overcome my previous challenges. I made it then; therefore, I can make it now."

- **Jermale Eddie**: Business Partnerships Manager – Amplify GR (Grand Rapids, MI); CEO – Malamiah Juice Bar – "As a CEO of two companies in the food/beverage industry, the last 2+ years have had their share of stressful days. To reduce stress and anxiety, I put on my headphones and listen to jazz. I also know when I need to take a nap, so this is another [way] to de-stress and sift through the anxiety. A few other things that I do, depending on what I have going on during the day are: going to the beach, getting out in nature, and sometimes I simply exhale and release the tension in my shoulders."

- **Phillip Gillam**: Director of Rates and Regulatory Affairs – Summit Utilities (Little Rock, AR) – "To relieve stress during the day, I'll periodically get up and take a walk around the building. Anxiety is a different problem that can manifest itself during the day, evening, or middle of the night. For that, I just try to get back to a calm place with deep breathing. Hope this helps."

- **Sheila McAfee**: Vice President/Compliance Risk Manager – MUFG Union Bank (DeSoto, TX) – "As a leader, in order to reduce stress and anxiety, I do several things. It all depends on the type of stress and anxiety I am experiencing. If it is work related, I take a break to try to get away from the situation and do deep breathing, work out with my trainer, or get in my hot tub with jets at a high level. If it is family stress, I have to pray, totally shut down sometimes for a day or so, and ask God to help me keep my cool. If it is self-inflicted stress and anxiety, I love to read nonfiction books or color in my many coloring books, which takes me to a realm of peacefulness. My favorite coloring books are centered around *Dumbo*, Tom & Jerry, the Looney Tunes, and *The Wizard of Oz*. Also, I am a firm believer in pampering myself with manicures, pedicures, and full body massages often. Most importantly, I have a wonderful spiritual psychologist whom I talk to regularly. If stress and anxiety aren't effectively managed, they can adversely impact the quality of our lives. Therefore, I try to eat balanced meals, get proper rest, exercise at least three times a week, drink alcohol moderately, and stay acutely aware of how my body feels and what my mind is saying to me. In other words, I try to stay in the present, be still, and listen"

- **Scott McGehee**: Co-owner/Chef at Heights Taco & Tamale Co.; Co-Owner/Chef at Lost Forty Brewing; and Co-Owner/Chef at Big Orange: Midtown (Little Rock, AR) – "To relieve the stress from the day, I typically get horizontal and watch TV! (My personal way to meditate/rest my mind). I work out at 6 a.m., seven days a week, which helps wake up my body and mind—and helps me navigate successfully throughout the day. When things are particularly difficult, I often take a ride on my motorcycle, which I find pretty liberating."

- **Roz Noble**: Retired elementary school educator (Charlotte, NC) – "I listen to classical music and get outside the city to commune in nature. If I cannot get outside the city, I sit outside and look at night skies or find bodies of water to sit near. On occasions I walk and listen to [the biblical book of] The Psalms. I disconnect from TV for days.

- **Sharon Reid**: People Relations Director – United Farm Workers (Keene, CA) – "Put virtual meditation sessions on the calendar. Get out a coloring book while on calls and color during the call. Take the dog for a walk or hold a walking meeting."

- **Ryan Rives**: Vice-President of Business Development – Centerpost Media (Arlington, TX) – "Work out or listen to a scientific or spiritual podcast to intentionally trigger a flow state."[30]

---

[30] A psychological term, "flow state" means to become fully immersed in whatever activity you are involved in at the moment, with little to no distraction.

- **Lee J. Yi**: Chaplain – United States Navy (Bremerton, WA) – "I just step outside and take a view of God's creation. The sound and sight of the ocean is very calming. Occasionally, you catch a glimpse of a whale or dolphins, as well."

Change: The Great Stressor

You've heard it before; I want you to hear it again: "People do not like change." Go ahead and write that down somewhere. And once you write it down, I want you to put a big X through it because it is absolutely *untrue*. It is a complete falsehood that people do not like change. What people do not like is *unexplained or poorly implemented change*. People are used to change, and they even expect a certain amount of regular change. It isn't change itself that creates stress, but the inadequate ways in which we implement or introduce change.

Think about any change that you have experienced in your life that just didn't go over well. It could have been a change on the job or even a change in your family structure. Maybe the employees didn't like it, maybe your family members didn't like it, maybe you didn't like it. Whatever the situation, I can guarantee that one of the reasons that change did not go over so well is that it was poorly explained or incorrectly implemented. The process is what creates stress, not the change itself.

As a leader, you will often be called upon to lead change. You may even be in the midst of some type of change in the workplace at this very moment. As a leader, you need to be able to skillfully navigate your team through change. And, since the best leaders are the best communicators, you've got to be able to communicate that change effectively.

There are three questions that must be asked and answered before implementing the change to properly prepare people for change with minimal stress. These **Three Essential Change Questions** appear below, in the order in which they should be asked and answered:

1. Why is this change necessary? If you do not have an answer for your people about why you or the organization will be making this change, *you are not yet ready to implement the change.*

People don't like unexplained change. If I knocked on your door and said, "Hello, I need you to come with me right now. Okay? Hey, stop staring at me—I need you to move! Get out, right now," you are going to resist. You will probably ask, "Who are you, and why do I need to leave my house?" You are not questioning me because you're being a jerk. The fault is mine. I failed to explain to you *why* I need you to make this change and leave your house. So, you're most likely going to resist me.

Let's try it again the right way. I knock on your door, and I say, "Hello, your home was built on a nuclear reactor about 10 years ago and it's going to explode in 10 minutes. I need you out, right now." Now, not only are you going to gladly leave the house, but you're probably going to kiss my ring and thank me for giving you the information. Do you see the difference? It wasn't that the person didn't want to change, but my communication that was the problem. I failed to give them the reason why.

Here are the criteria I use to determine if a change is in fact necessary:

- Does your organization's stated vision or mission match your current practices? In other words, are you doing what you say you believe you should do? For example, if one of your organizational values is giving five-star customer service for your clients but you spend tons of time dealing with unhappy customers, it's probably time to make some serious changes in your organizational practices.
- Solicit regular input from your employees who do the work of the organization.

  Are there many complaints? Are there suggestions for ways to streamline activities or increase effectiveness? If so, then it's time to make some changes.

- Regularly get feedback from your clients or customers. Ask them this simple question:

"How can we serve you better?" If you find some uniformity in their suggestions to you, then it's time for change. Without your clientele, you cease to exist."

- Are our current practices keeping current with technological trends, or are we still doing things the way they were done five or ten years ago? For example, one of my clients—a large network of early childhood development centers—recently invested lots of money into installing smart boards into their classrooms and providing students with electronic tablets. The impetus behind this change was that once their students graduated and went to elementary school, that type of technology was commonplace. Their students had no idea how to utilize that technology, which automatically put them behind once they got into the public-school classrooms.

So, the first question you must ask and answer if you're going to be a leader who successfully helps an organization change is "Why is this change necessary?"

2. What will this change require that I or we do differently? I regularly provide company-wide workforce training in a certain organization's areas of customer service and communication skills. The executive leadership team had recently made a major change in their accounting software program. Part of this change in accounting software meant that the employees would have to do more paperwork—much more paperwork. That didn't go over well, and I'm sure you know why. Nobody from the executive team who made the decision had told the employees that this new accounting program would require more paperwork to be completed whenever there was a request for supplies or funds for any reason at any time.

If people had been informed in advance, "Okay, we're going to get new software, but part of this change requires that we do more paperwork," it would have gone more smoothly. I'm not suggesting everybody would have been in love with the change, but I do know that there would have been less drama and less of a mutiny had they been forewarned about the effects of the change. The employees would have been more prepared for it. Instead, they were uninformed; thus, they were caught by surprise, and reacted negatively.

Part of what you've got to do as a leader is help people to understand, "Once we make this change, this is what you/we will need to do differently as a result." You've got to prepare people for change. The more prepared they are, the less resistant they will be and the less stressed they will be.

3. What will happen to us/you/me if we *fail* to make this change?

This is the question that helps you achieve what we often call "buy-in" from people, especially those who have a habit of fighting change. This is where you paint the bleakest picture you can paint while still being honest. Think about what could go wrong if either you or the organization fail to make this change. The answer to this question is what's going to help those people who are resistant to change to be a bit more on board.

For example, let's revisit the organization that made the disastrous rollout of the new accounting software. For those who absolutely hated the idea of implementing new software and doing more paperwork, it may have been helpful to explain it this way:

"Okay, I understand that this change sounds like it will be one big headache. But last year, because of accounting discrepancies with our federal government contracts, our company was fined six figures in penalties. That money had to come from somewhere and is part of the reason we were unable to give cost of living increases to each of our employees. We simply cannot afford to lose six figures every year. This new accounting software, though it requires more paperwork on the front end, allows us to be much more accurate, and prevents us from losing money that we cannot afford to lose."

Now of course, you would not tell your employees anything like that unless it was true. But, once people see that the change really is for the greater good, they are less reluctant to curse it. You will never have 100 percent satisfaction with any change, but you can decrease the possibility of a violent insurrection by answering this question for them. You can even say to them, "Okay, we can keep things the way they are right now, but if we keep things the way they are in the long term, here's what's going to happen—and I'm sure you don't want this."

Those are three questions you must ask and answer for your people to ensure that change is not more stressful than it needs to be. And I repeat, if you do not have clearly explained, honest answers for your people concerning whatever change you're trying to implement, *the change is premature.* You're not ready to implement change until you can provide your people with answers to these questions.

Wrap-Up

In this chapter, we have seen:
- The startling prevalence of stress in the workplace, and the negative effects it can have on one's body and emotional well-being.
- Five detailed tips for successfully managing stress on the job and even at home.
- Why organizational change creates stress, and the Three Essential Questions that must be asked and answered to prevent that from happening.

Focusing on making the right decisions will result in a less stressful tenure in leadership. In addition, we have gotten extremely specific about strategies for decreasing work-related stress. There is yet another tactic wise leaders employ that will reduce their stress levels: creating shortcuts to effectiveness. Since having the right focus helps you waste less time, thus making it easier for you to accomplish more for your organization more quickly, the next chapter will equip you to create results faster and reduce your learning curve. The goal is to help you become the most effective leader possible without wasting time that you really do not have.

Chapter 3 Implementation Tasks:

1. Schedule and attend regular appointments with a therapist.

2. Find – or rediscover – a hobby and regularly enjoy it.

3. Begin scheduling down-time on your calendar and ask everyone to respect that time.

4. Start exercising regularly. Schedule it, just as you will schedule your down-time.

5. Spend time with non-workplace friends.

6. Look at the four criteria to help you determine if in fact a change within your organization is necessary and do the suggested work to make that determination. If any of those criteria apply to you, begin to implement the necessary changes only after you...

7. Ask and answer each of the Three Essential Change Questions.

Chapter 3 Reactions:

1. What did I already know?

2. Of what was I reminded? How will I act upon those reminders?

3. What was brand new information to me?

Shortcuts To Effectiveness:
Reducing Your Leadership Learning Curve

It bears repeating: those who hired you or appointed you are expecting to see results quickly. While I believe learning from the right person or the right source is never a waste of time, the amount of time you have available for on-the-job learning will not be as long as you had hoped—nor should it be. What separates strong leaders from the rest of the pack is our ability to quickly size up a situation and make a wise, well-informed decision while also juggling other responsibilities. That's not easy to do, and that's why leadership is not for everybody.

Imagine you are on an airplane that is about to make an emergency landing. Which leader would you rather have in this moment—Leader A or Leader B?

Here is Leader A's approach:

"Okay, everyone. It looks like we are about to be forced to make a crash landing. First, let me take a survey. Show of hands please: how many of you think we should probably get some parachutes ready and prepare the emergency exits, and other things like that? Come on; get your hands up high so I can count. Let's see, that's 1…2…3…4… Ma'am, is your hand up or down? I can't tell…okay…5…6…"

Contrast that with Leader B's approach:

> "Folks, we're about to make an emergency landing. Follow my instructions and we will all make it through this situation safely. First, we need to do this…"

Both leaders were attempting to help, but the one who would earn your confidence would be the Leader B, who was decisive and quick in their response to the impending difficulty. And notice: Leader B didn't feel the need to yell, scream, or shout profanities; rather, Leader B made it very clear that they were trained for such a time as this, and that you would be wise to follow them.

I can hear some of your thoughts as you read these words: "Derrick, are you sure? I don't think I'm ready yet. I need just a little more time." But as Napoleon Hill once said: "Don't wait; the time will never be just right."[31]

Emerging leader, you can do this. Right now. Some leaders overthink to the point of inaction, but you should never use learning as an excuse for inaction. There comes a time in leadership when you just must step up, take the mantle of responsibility, trust yourself, and say, "Follow my instructions and we will all make it through this situation safely." Emerging leaders, to be as effective as possible as soon as possible, must employ specific tactics that are designed to shorten one's leadership learning curve.

In Chapter 2, I shared with you two of my five suggested methods for shortening your leadership learning curve:

1. **Getting to know the abilities and attitudes of each employee you lead; and**
2. **Knowing that the #1 key to motivating your workforce is helping them to discover the deeper purpose of the work that they do.**

---

[31] https://www.brainyquote.com/authors/napoleon-hill-quotes

3. I decided to share those two methods in that particular portion of the book because they both fall under the same overarching category of **focusing on the right details**.

4. In this chapter, you will learn the remaining three methods for shortening your learning curve. To introduce our deeper dive into these next three methods, I list them below and give the rationale for each one. I think you will see why they are included in this chapter which focuses on shaving time off one's leadership learning curve.

5. **Becoming an exceptionally skilled communicator.** Everything one does as a leader emanates from or revolves around communication skills. For example, how will employees know the vision or mission of the organization? The leader must communicate it. What is excellent customer service, if it isn't communicating well with those who benefit from the work that you do? How will your employees learn of your expectations of them? Those expectations must be communicated in some effective manner.

6. **Having the right support team in your corner.** One of the fastest ways to get where you're going is to be guided by someone who has already successfully made the same journey you are now attempting to make; and

7. **Mastering the fine art of delegation.** This skill will exponentially multiply your impact as a leader. You can't do everything by yourself, nor should you. Delegation is a skill all strong leaders need to develop.

Let's get to it!

Becoming An Exceptionally Skilled Communicator

Graduates of Stanford Business School call communication skills the most important thing they learned during their entire time as students. In fact, they said it was also the biggest determining factor not only in their success on the job, but also in their subsequent promotions on the job.

As my former coach and current mentor Patricia Fripp is fond of saying, "It never ceases to amaze me that intelligent, well-educated, and ambitious people frequently overlook developing the number one skill that is guaranteed to position them ahead of the crowd: the ability to communicate eloquently and with confidence."[32] Making the conscious decision to become a stellar communicator is perhaps the best way to shorten your learning curve and implementations of change. Unclear communication leads to unnecessary repetition, which robs you of precious time and slows down your efforts at fomenting change. Poor communication leads to lost time, frustrated employees, low morale, missed performance goals, and ineffective leadership. Time spent re-explaining, correcting, and clarifying yourself is time that would be better spent casting vision, solving problems, or making other decisions that can move the organization forward.

Harvard Business School says on this subject:

> "A leader is someone who inspires positive, incremental change by empowering those around them to work toward common objectives. A leader's most powerful tool for doing so is communication.

---

[32] Patricia Fripp, "Preparing and Presenting Powerful Talks," (audio lecture, Toastmasters International, circa 2000).

Effective communication is vital to gain trust, align efforts in the pursuit of goals, and inspire positive change. When communication is lacking, important information can be misinterpreted, causing relationships to suffer and, ultimately, creating barriers that hinder progress."[33]

According to Tom Starner, a renowned business writer who focuses on human resources:

"Much of a team's success lies in the pattern of connection a leader has with direct reports, and the way [they] empower them to extend that pattern down the line, and so on. In a business environment that is woefully lacking in employee commitment, leaders who aren't actively connecting with people are themselves a liability."[34]

Stellar communication is therefore perhaps the most important skill for a leader to work toward mastering. The more skilled you are in the art of communication, the better you will be at connecting with those whom you lead. The stronger the connection to your employees becomes, the greater the benefits to your performance, your career, and your future in leadership.

Here, we first need to discuss a few points about the link between effective leadership and stellar communication skills.

1. Communicating well is the one critical skill that 91 percent of the workforce says their current leader lacks.[35] If leaders do not communicate well, the directions they give will be unclear and

---

[33] https://online.hbs.edu/blog/post/leadership-communication#:~:text=A%20leader%20is%20someone%20who,goals%2C%20and%20inspire%20positive%20change.

[34] Tom Starner, Survey: Boss' bad communication skills drag the company down. HR Dive. June 25, 2015. https://www.hrdive.com/news/survey-bosss-bad-communication-skills-drag-the-company-down/401263/

[35] Marcel Schwantes, Survey: 91 Percent of 1,000 Employees Say Their Bosses Lack This 1 Critical Skill. Inc.com. https://www.inc.com/marcel-schwantes/survey-91-percent-of-1000-employees-say-their-boss.html

their expectations will not be met. With unclear directions and unmet expectations, workforce performance inevitably suffers. Thus, leaders who do not communicate well end up killing the morale of the people who follow their leadership. Meeting with employees, whether individually or in groups, requires excellent communication. Providing feedback and constructive criticism to the people you lead requires excellent communication. Recognizing stellar employee performances - which in turn boosts workplace morale - requires excellent communication. Ineffective leaders often substitute micromanaging for excellent communication, which negatively impacts the morale of those being micromanaged.

Effective leaders are skilled at articulating the direction in which the organization must move and convincing others to move in that direction. Without a clear direction and a sense of team unity, the organizational output will be subpar at best and abysmal at worst. The most effective leaders are indeed the most effective communicators.

2. On the other hand, communicators that cannot lead can *tell* you where to go, but they cannot take you there. Imagine that you are describing for your family or your friends the ideal vacation that you are all going to take. You begin describing for them the places they're going to go, the sights they're going to see, the delicious food they're going to enjoy, the culture they're going to encounter, and all the things they're going to learn. You get them so excited about this trip—but you're unable to take them on the trip. You can describe it for them, but you can't get them there.

You got them excited about this wonderful journey and you told them all the signposts along the way, but now you can't get them there. So, they are defeated and deflated. If you are a communicator who cannot lead, you are doing the exact same thing to the people who are trying to follow your leadership. You may be able to describe the vision. You may be able to talk to them about where this organization should be. But if you don't have the critical leadership skills that will get them from A to B, you've gotten them excited, but you have failed them—and now they are defeated and deflated. Communication and leadership go hand in hand.

3. A leader that cannot communicate reduces their leadership potential. If a communicator who cannot lead can get you excited but you end up being defeated, then a leader who cannot communicate reduces their leadership potential. Anything you want to do well as a leader involves communication, so if communication is a weak point, you cannot be a strong leader.

Let's say you are the leader of an organization and you're trying to get better at customer service. Well, what *is* customer service? It's communication, so to improve it, you will want to improve your team's communication. You will cover topics like:

- How do we deal with angry customers?
- What do we say to angry customers?
- What are the things that we say and do to get customers excited and get them coming back?
- How do we get people to tell others about our organization, whether we are for profit or not for profit?

All those skills involve communication! So, if you are a leader who cannot communicate well, how are you going to teach your team to improve at customer service?

Let me remind you of the lesson you have already learned about the importance of the leader skillfully navigating organizational change. Leading an organization through any type of change is, at its core, all about communication. Consider the following questions:

- How are you going to get people to understand what this change is all about?
- How are you going to get them excited about the change?
- How are you going to help them to understand that this change is necessary?

- What are you going to do to help them to understand what will happen to them if they don't follow through on these changes?

All those questions will be answered via some channel of communication!

Leadership and communication go hand in hand. If you're a leader who cannot communicate, you limit your leadership potential. Luckily...

4. Effective communication is a skill that can be learned and improved upon. Take heart, those of you who are thinking, "Oh my gosh, I'm a terrible communicator, I must be a horrible leader!" Leadership is a skill that can be learned and improved upon, and so is communication.

People often say leaders are born, not made. That's partially true. Some leadership qualities are innate, but communication is a skill you can learn and improve upon if you have the right partner and the right coach...or book.

Tips For Better Verbal and Nonverbal Communication

Communication is much more than words. I want you to participate in a little experiment with me. I want you to say aloud the word, "Sure." The first time you say it, I want you to say the word, "Sure" like you're happy. Go ahead and do it now. Next, I want you to say the word "Sure" like you're angry. Go ahead and do it now. Finally, I want you to say the word "Sure" again, but this time, I want you to say the word sarcastically. Go ahead.

Did you hear the difference? It was the same word, but by changing your tone—and changing your facial expressions and body language—the message itself changed.

You see, communication is not just words. You can say the right thing but say it the wrong way.

Let's cover the three main types of communication:

- Verbal communication,
- Nonverbal communication, and
- Written communication.

Verbal Communication

1. Words are the most obvious form of communication, and the goal in communication is for your words to be clearly understood. However, did you know that more than 50 percent of US citizens read below a fifth-grade level?[36] This does not mean speaking to your employees as if you are speaking to a room of elementary students. It simply means that skilled communicators strive to make sure that their communication is more about imparting necessary information in an accessible manner than it is about impressing others with one's vocabulary.

For example, when I'm speaking to a diverse crowd, instead of, "I want to speak to you about your epistemological stance," I would probably say, "I want to spend some time talking to you about the different ways in which people learn." I would deliver the same message, but with a more accessible vocabulary.

Clearly, I am not saying that people who do not have graduate level degrees are ignorant—that is definitely not the case. I know many non-degreed people who have much more sense than some people with many letters behind their names. However, I *am* saying that your goal as a communicator is not to impress people. Again,

---

[36] Emily Schmidt, Reading the numbers: 130 million american adults have low literacy skills, but funding differs drastically by state. American Public Media. March 16, 2022. https://www.apmresearchlab.org/10x-adult-literacy

your goal, in communication, is to be understood. I contend that if the recipient did not understand you, then you did not communicate!

2. Tone is one level of communication with which most leaders make big mistakes. Over the years, I have had many leaders who come to me for leadership coaching or speech coaching say, "Dr. Noble people are angry with me and there's a mutiny on my hands. What's the problem? I only said what needed to be said."

My immediate response is always the same: "Perhaps the problem was the *way* you said it."

Communication is not just *what* you say, it's how you *sound* when you say it.

For example, let's practice speaking aloud just as we did earlier with the word "sure." Your significant other comes to you and says, "You haven't told me you love me lately." Read the following response aloud in a soft, remorseful tone:

"Babe, I'm sorry. I've been so busy. I love you. I love you. Okay?"

Now, read those exact same words in a frustrated, exasperated, almost angry tone:

"Babe, I'm sorry. I've been so busy. I love you. I love you. Okay?"

Did you hear the difference? Same words, but the message changed because of the tone. Some of us need to practice what we say before we say it to people, because that's the reason they may neither like our leadership nor us. It's not just words; it's tone.

Nonverbal Communication

1. Body movement and positioning. It's not just what you say. It's not just how you sound. It's also *how you look* when you're communicating. This involves the way you move your body, the way you gesture, and your facial expressions. Your body speaks even when your mouth does not.

A few years ago, I was coaching a young lady who had just become an executive at a major corporation. In fact, she was the very first female vice president in the history of that organization. She contacted me via my LinkedIn page and asked me to be her leadership coach. When we met face-to-face, she began our session by saying to me, "I have broken the glass ceiling as the first female VP. Soon, I will be speaking at my first meeting as vice president, and I need to make a great impression. Will you work with me on my script?"

I enthusiastically responded, "I'll gladly work with you on your script. Before we do that, I want you to practice walking into the room."

She was puzzled, and asked, "Why do I need to practice walking into the room? I need you to work with me on my *script.*"

I replied, "I first need you to understand that you begin to communicate before you ever open your mouth. If you walk into the room with your head down, what you're communicating is, 'I'm not confident.' If you walk into your room with too overconfident of a gait, what you're communicating is, 'Everyone here is beneath me. You're all peasants.' So, I need you to practice walking into the room with confidence."

We practiced her body language before we ever practiced any word that was to come out of her mouth. For example, I noticed that she tended to slouch a bit when she walked. When I pointed that out to her, she admitted, "I was always the tallest girl in class growing up, and my classmates called me 'The Giraffe.' I started slouching as a result." Before I could respond to her admission, she quickly added, "But I'm not an awkward young girl anymore, am I? Okay - got it." She immediately straightened her posture and walked with the confidence of a high-ranking executive.

I later noted that she often made harsh, penetrating pointing gestures with her index finger as she was speaking. Though her company was headquartered in the United States, it had many international branches. In many European, African, and Latin American nations, gesturing with one's index finger is at best impolite and at worst rude. In many Asian countries, it is especially rude - and her company's largest branch was in Japan! We worked on her emphasizing points with tone - like including more vocal inflection - rather than with pointing gestures. She finally began to understand that communication is not just what you say or how you sound, but how you look.

2. Facial expressions. Have you ever seen anyone whose face seemed to say, "Approach me and die"? I have. In fact, I'll share a funny encounter with you. I live in Baldwin Hills, a suburb of Los Angeles often referred to as "Black Beverly Hills" because of the numbers of African American celebrities who live in the area. As you might imagine, celebrities are often recognized and approached by adoring fans. But there was one famous neighbor whom nobody approached—ever.

I would occasionally see internationally renowned actor Samuel L. Jackson at the Ralph's grocery store just blocks from my home, but nobody would ever approach him. Do you know why? While I'm sure Mr. Jackson is a very nice man, his facial expression made it very clear that he did not want to be bothered. He looked as if he would body slam you if you said hello to him. I often imagined that he was thinking to himself, "Where are the #$%* eggs?! I need the #$%* eggs!"

Your facial expressions can communicate warmth and approachability, or they can communicate that you do not wish to be bothered. As I am often fond of saying, "If you're happy and you know it, tell your face." I suggest that you stand in front of a mirror and practice greeting your employees and work colleagues. Often, in your head you think you are looking pleasant, but you look as if you can't find the eggs.

I remember sharing this once at a company-wide training session I was conducting in Fresno, California. One of the attendees admitted aloud - and I will make her language a bit more PG - "Yeah, that sounds like me. They tell me I have Resting Witch Face. Everyone says I look like I could snap at any moment. But I really am a nice person. What should I do?" I gave her three practical suggestions which I now pass along to you:

- Keep a mirror at your desk and check your face in it occasionally to be sure that you look as approachable and as pleasant as you would like to.
- Have a "facial accountability partner" who will occasionally poke their head into your cubicle and let you know how happy or angry you look, and
- Pause occasionally throughout the day and think about something - or someone - that makes you happy. Think about a significant other or think about a funny joke you heard recently. Think about something for which you are thankful or grateful. Doing so will most likely change your mood, and your face will follow.

A few months later, when I returned to conduct another training for that group, our Resting Witch Face friend was there and proudly said to me, "Hey - it works. I didn't even notice just how nasty I looked until I tried those suggestions. I scared myself whenever I looked in the mirror, so I made the necessary adjustments."

People often notice your face before they hear a word that comes out of your mouth, so take those suggestions and work on improving your facial expressions.

3. Physical Appearance/Dress. The phrase "dress for success" really does seem to be good advice. Studies have shown that workplace attire plays a significant role in employees' perceptions of themselves and their organization's culture.[37] To quote Ethan Surrett - a scholar, MBA student, and graduate assistant at the University of Southern Mississippi - who has conducted research about workplace attire:

"In occupations and workplaces requiring more sociable attributes, workers must be perceived as friendly, courteous, and approachable and must possess all other sociable qualities. In these cases, casual dress may be more appropriate as it elicits many of these feelings in the employee. However, a worker in a high-ranking position would represent the company, thereby molding the company's image, so this worker can be perceived as being essential or powerful and, in theory, should dress in formal attire to perceive themselves as such."[38]

The implications of such studies make a convincing argument that one's attire in the workplace affects one's mindset, which in turn can positively impact one's job performance. Some quick tips I often give to leaders concerning one's physical appearance are:

- Become familiar with your organization's dress code, if one exists, and dress slightly above what is expected of you. For example, if the dress code says, "business casual", I recommend stepping it up a notch and dressing "smart casual", which is "a dress code that combines well-fitting, polished business wear with elements of casual attire— think blouses, polo shirts, button-downs, chinos, dress pants, dark-wash jeans, and polished, practical footwear."[39]
- Make sure your clothing fits you well and is neither too tight nor too loose. I will never forget how apprehensive I was when a nurse's aide that was supposed to take a blood sample from me tripped over the pant legs on her scrubs,

---

[37] Ethan Surrett, "How Workplace Attire Affects Employee Perceptions and Organizational Culture" (honors thesis, University of Southern Mississippi, 2021), iv, https://aquila.usm.edu/cgi/viewcontent.cgi?article=1784&context=honors_theses

[38] Ibid, 10.

[39] https://www.masterclass.com/articles/smart-casual-dress-code-and-attire-guide

because they were too long and ill fitting. I said to myself, "If she can't walk without tripping, I'm not about to let her come near me with that needle!"

- Your clothing doesn't need to be expensive, but it does need to be clean and nicely pressed. I'm a firm believer, as some of the studies suggest, that attire impacts attitude which in turn impacts performance. Sloppy dress, sloppy performance. Use that iron or, if you prefer, have your clothing dry cleaned regularly. And bear in mind there are plenty of clothing options that will not break your bank account but will help you look polished and professional.

Practice these tips for better verbal and nonverbal communication, and make sure they are congruent with one another. Confident words in a timid voice accompanied by careless body language combined with an angry face and disheveled clothing confuses your audience and weakens your credibility._

Tips For Better Written Communication

A few years ago, some good friends of mine who had been married for just a few years moved with their two small children to a small new town, an hour's drive away from their previous, large, urban setting. As is sometimes the case in smaller towns, word traveled fast about the new family. One of the three preschools in that small community decided to send my friends some information about their preschool via snail mail.

The preschool mailed them a letter and a brochure. The letter spelled "school" as: "S-H-O-O-L." Wait—there's more. Here are the exact words from the brochure, in the exact way in which they were written.

"Welcome to the neighborhood. We want your kids to be apart of our family; this will be there home away from home."

"Apart" means "separate from." What the preschool should have typed was "a part." And the word "there" should have been written as the possessive pronoun "their."

What do you think my friends did with that letter and that brochure? Not only did they throw them away, but they decided, "We are never going to send our kids to that place."

Organizations often ask me to conduct workforce training on how to improve their employees' writing skills. Let's face it: many of us have been out of school for a long time. We may not remember the difference between an adverb and an adjective. We may not know the difference between "who" and "whom," "fewer" and "less," "farther" and "further," and so on.

As a leader, part of your responsibility is going to be to communicate in the written form, and if what you have written down is full of grammatical errors—or if it is simply unclear or does not make sense—you are going to short-circuit your communication. I want to make a few points about written communication:

1. Communication has not really occurred until your recipient has understood you. That is equally true of spoken communication and written communication. Verbally, the listener is the recipient. With written communication, the reader is the recipient. If your reader does not understand what you have written, you have failed to communicate. Remember, communication is not simply dispensing information; communication means making sure that the information you sent was understood. I'll give you a few practical tips here to ensure your writing is easier to understand and less clunky:

- Use the most familiar, accessible words. A huge mistake that many people make in communication is using big words when simpler ones will do. The goal is not to impress; the goal is to be understood. If you think collegiate-level words are needed in order to get your point across, bear this in mind: the Gettysburg Address, which many historians consider to have been one of the greatest orations ever, contains only 271 words, 251 of which have only one or two syllables.[40] In this case, what works for the spoken word also works for the written word.

• Simplify your sentences. Why use 20 words when five will get your point across just as well? Remember, your reader is often just as busy as you are. They will appreciate you much more if your communication with them saves them as much time as possible. For example, instead of writing:

"Please be aware that the length of time that XYZ Corporation allows for scheduled breaks throughout the day should be no more than a maximum of 15 minutes", try writing it this way:

"Scheduled breaks are 15 minutes."

We rewrote a 28-word sentence as a five-word sentence and still managed to communicate the same point.

You can also trim some common phrases. For instance, "due to the fact that…" can simply be written as "since." Here is a before and after example:

"Due to the fact that it's raining, we will reschedule
our outdoor lunch on the grounds."

"*Since* it's raining, we will reschedule today's outdoor lunch."

Also, "In the event that…" can be rewritten as "If…" There are many times when brevity can be substituted for unnecessary, frivolous linguistic erudition. See what I did there?

Here is a homework assignment for you. Go back through some of your work emails from the past month or so and look for any

---

[40] Stephen E. Lucas, The Art of Public Speaking (New York: McGrawiHill, 2012, 11th ed.), 225.

sentences longer than 12 words or so. Rewrite each one so that it has a maximum of five words. You will be surprised at how easily you can get the same point across with fewer words.

- Stop using cliches. A cliche is a phrase or opinion that is overused and could potentially be misunderstood. For example, I often heard this phrase when I was growing up: "Let's throw this against the wall and see if it sticks." Many years later, I said that to a group of young leaders in their 20s, all of whom looked as if I had suddenly started speaking a foreign language. My message would have been much clearer had I simply said, "Let's try this and see if it works."

Our language is filled with similar cliches that people who didn't grow up when and where we did may not understand. Check your writing for cliches, such as "There's more than one way to skin a cat," "Can we hash this thing out," or "Put that in your pipe and smoke it." Rewrite them in clearer, more succinct language.

- Use the buddy system and have a colleague read your material before you send it. I am aware of a company that has what they call the "Six-Eye Rule." It means that at least three different people need to read any written materials (emails, letters, etc.) before they are sent. This is a fantastic way to ensure both clarity and readability.

After reading this first point and its subpoints, some might say, "Well, I wrote what needed to be written. I said what needed to be said. If they didn't get it, that's on them." This is incorrect! If your recipient doesn't "get it," the fault lies with you, because:

2. The obligation of the writer is to guide my reader into a clear understanding. Whenever I speak of clarity in written communication, someone inevitably asks, "Well, what do you mean by clarity? Are you talking about details?"

Yes, whenever I speak of clarity, I'm talking about details—but I'm also talking about *word choice*. For example, let's say you are trying to sell a car. Writing in a newspaper ad, "Cheap car for sale," will make the reader think the car is of inferior quality. A better word choice—and, what you intended to communicate about the car— would be *affordable*. When you are writing, try to put yourself in the reader's shoes, and pay attention to how each word makes you feel. If a word gives off the wrong emotion, try a different one that has a similar meaning (a thesaurus could help you, here!). Using the word cheap, instead of using the word affordable, creates a negative mood, which leads to third point:

To further drive home this point about guiding the reader into a clear understanding, I want to share a tip with you that I often share with writers. Before you hit send on that email or that text message, or before you send that letter, read it aloud and ask yourself this question: "Is there a possibility that what I've written could be misunderstood?" If the answer is yes, then what you've written is not clear enough. Go back and rewrite it. If there is a possibility that your written communication could be misunderstood, it is not yet ready to be sent. Again, your goal as the writer is to make sure that your reader has a very clear understanding of your message. And if you think there's a possibility it might not be clear, rewrite it until it *is* clear.

For example, you send the following email to one of your employees:

"Good morning. We should discuss job performance soon. Thanks."

This email raises more questions than it answers, and that is always a sign of unclear communication. Here are the questions your employee will most likely ask after reading that message:

1. Who will be in on this discussion: just me and the supervisor or others? Who is the "we"?
2. Whose job performance are we discussing: mine? My supervisor's? My colleagues'?
3. Is the job performance we need to discuss satisfactory, or is it unsatisfactory?
4. When exactly is "soon"? Within the next hour? Before the end of the day? Within the next week?"

Take this opportunity to practice clearer communication. Rewrite that unclear email in the space below until any possible questions from the reader have been proactively addressed.

_____

_____

_____

Let's practice this skill of clear communication a little bit more. What comes to your mind when you read the following sentences?

1. Thanks for your order, Ms. Garcia. Your package will arrive shortly.
2. You ought to understand what I'm saying.
3. You'd better get this to me before 3:00.

Rewrite each sentence using clearer, more professional words and tone:

1.
2.
3.

Here is another tip I often share with leaders concerning their writing. Remember we shared earlier that words can either create a positive mood or a negative mood. To keep your writing a bit more positive, try writing from the point of view of possibility vs. impossibility. For example, instead of saying "Our office closes at 4:00", rewrite it to say, "For your convenience, our office is open until 4:00." The first message focuses upon what will not or cannot happen, while the second message focuses upon what will or can happen, thus altering the mood of the sentence. Get it?

Now it's your turn; rewrite each sentence
below with more positive language:

1. We cannot open your checking account for any less than $1,000.

2. The financial consultant cannot see you today or tomorrow.

3. Your child does not have all their paperwork completed to enroll in our program.

Exceptional writing skills are essential in leadership. I passionately believe that the best leaders are also the best communicators. I strongly recommend that you take a brush-up course or two in grammar and business writing. I often provide these types of trainings online and in person for my business clients, and there are also some seminar companies that provide full-day or half-day courses specifically designed to help business leaders become better communicators. Don't allow unprofessional written communication to keep you from advancing in your career.

Let us now move to a discussion of yet another form of communication; one that most people fail to even consider as communication: listening.

Leaders Are Listeners

"Effective listening is actively absorbing the information given to you by a speaker, showing that you are listening and interested, and providing feedback to the speaker so that he or she knows the message was received." – Dr. Scott Williams, Wright State University.[41]

One of the most frequent complaints employees share with me is that their managers and supervisors are extremely poor listeners. Too often, leaders begin to search for answers without carefully listening to their team members describe the problem. Employees often become angry or despondent quickly when they feel they have not been heard.

A few years ago, I was asked to facilitate a discussion at a large church located in a community that was rapidly changing, and whose membership numbers were quickly declining. While the regular members and attendees were middle class to wealthy and in their 50s and older, the neighborhood was rapidly gaining working class and lower income residents, many of whom were in their 30s and younger. A public housing development had recently been erected just two blocks from the church's building. Despite living so close to the church, none of those young families—or any other young people living in that community—were attending the church services.

One evening, the leadership team of one of the community health organizations in that neighborhood partnered with leaders of the church to host a dialogue, one of the aims of which was to discuss ways for the church and the new, younger residents of the neighborhood to interact with one another. Since I pride myself on being comfortable with facilitating dialogue, I gladly accepted

---

[41] Scott Williams, Listening Effectively. Wright State University. http://www.wright.edu/~scott.williams/LeaderLetter/listening.htm#:~:text=Research%20has%20found%20that%20by,in%20the%20people%20you%20manage.

the invitation to lead the discussion. After everyone in attendance grabbed plates of cookies and potato chips, I opened the proceedings by asking if anyone had a question or a comment about how the organizations in the community could work together for the good of the neighborhood. An older attendee asked one of the young residents of the housing development about why he had not yet come to visit the church.

The young man, who I assumed to have been in his 20s, respectfully explained: "I don't own a suit and tie, so I honestly figured you all wouldn't accept me. It's obvious to me by the kinds of cars I see in your parking lot on Sunday mornings that you folks are pretty well-to-do. Me, I drive an older Toyota, and I dress like the music I listen to: hip hop. And that's another question I have: what type of music do y'all sing? The only church music I know is Kirk Franklin. They play his stuff on hip hop stations. That's how I know him."

As he began talking about his love for hip-hop music, one of the older church leaders interrupted him and yelled at me, saying, "Dr. Noble, you're not giving us any answers or solutions! You're just standing there, listening. Why are we even here?" He then turned his ire to the young man he had interrupted. "And to you, young man, we're not about to play rap music in the church just to get people like you to come in."

Immediately, the young man sighed, looked back at the older gentleman, and said, "See, *that's* why I ain't coming. Y'all can't even listen—and you're always angry." He then dropped his paper plate of chocolate chip cookies and potato chips onto the table, began walking toward the exit door, and said, "When you're ready to hear what I have to say, come talk to me. Unit 1A, right on the corner. Peace."

At this point, I stepped in to prevent what I felt was about to quickly devolve into a fight. I said to the older gentleman, "How can we talk about solutions when we haven't yet heard what the problem is? Solutions come as a result of listening. Your opportunity to make a difference just walked out the door."

What that older leader and so many others like him—young and old and everything in between—fail to realize is that listening is a form of respect. When people feel respected, they tend to engage. When they feel disrespected, they tend to shut down—or even leave the situation, like that young man did. That church, the community organizations and the people who live within that community never came for any activity or event after that day. I wish the story had ended differently but let that be a lesson: you cannot establish rapport or connect with anyone if you don't demonstrate your respect for them by listening to them.

One can never be an effective leader if one is not also an active listener—and yes, I did say "never." Here are some tips that will help you to become the type of leader who quickly earns respect:

1. Demonstrate your listening skills by paraphrasing. After someone says something to you, and *before* you respond to it or attempt to solve the problem (if there is one), paraphrase what they just said to you to make sure you are both on the same page. For example:

Rosa: Derrick, I am feeling so overwhelmed with all these projects I'm trying to handle simultaneously. I don't think I'm going to finish the Simpson file on time. I may need another week.

Derrick: Okay, so just to be sure I'm following: you feel you have too much on your plate right now, and you don't think you will be able to complete the Simpson project on time. Sounds like you need me to help reduce your workload so you're not so overwhelmed. Is that correct?

This approach accomplishes two especially important tasks:

a) It demonstrates to Rosa that I was listening and, more importantly, that I *understood* what she was saying to me. If you can paraphrase someone's words into your own, you have demonstrated that you have fully grasped their message. b) It gives Rosa the opportunity to correct me if I have misinterpreted her. Had I missed her meaning, she could have replied, "Oh no, that's not what I mean. What I'm really trying to say is…" Paraphrasing goes a long way toward mutual understanding and toward letting the listener know that you are fully engaged in the conversation, both of which can lead to a satisfying solution.

2. Make consistent eye contact. Take this suggestion with a grain of salt because the idea that someone is actively listening to you if they are making direct eye contact is a very US-centric idea. In other parts of the world, and even in some ethnic cultures within the US, eye contact is considered disrespectful. Someone very close to me who is of Mexican heritage told me of the times he was scolded by his father for having made direct eye contact with him. "In my family, if a parent is instructing you or correcting you, to make eye contact is to *challenge* that parent. When your parents speak, you look down—never directly into their eyes."

So, do understand that this tip has some cultural variances—but connection can often be established between speakers when direct eye contact is made. Beyond eye contact, you should always try your best to look as engaged as possible. Remember, communication is not just what you say – it's how you look.

3. Do not multitask. Hey you, put your cell phone down and re-read this point! Seriously, though most of us fancy ourselves to be experts at multitasking, the truth is that very few of us can engage in more than one task simultaneously while giving each task equal attention. So really: put your phone down, turn your body away from your computer screen when a colleague comes into your office, and physically focus on them and them alone.

4. Remember and recall details from previous conversations. I must admit that I am not particularly good at this, but I try to improve upon it all the time. People who can recall previous details from previous conversations with you endear themselves to you.

I was once invited to speak at a business convention in Palm Springs, California. As I was checking in at the front desk, the hotel manager, Christopher, was handling the process for me. He noticed that, as I was placing my bag onto the floor, I winced in pain. I was having one of my occasional back spasms. Christopher said to me, "Dr. Noble, it looks like you're having some back pain. I'll tell you what: I'll re-assign you to a really nice suite here on the ground floor so you don't have to worry about carrying your luggage in and out of elevators or up and down the stairs."

I thanked him profusely. At that moment, a hotel employee wheeled a room service tray past me, filled with desserts. As I looked at the chocolate chip cheesecake (my all-time favorite dessert) on the tray, I muttered, "Wow."

Christopher said, "Oooooh, cheesecake fan, huh, Dr. Noble? Be sure to order one before the restaurant closes. There—you're all checked in. Enjoy your stay."

Nine months later, I was back in Palm Springs for a different event and checked into the same hotel. Guess who noticed me as soon as I walked into the lobby.

"Dr. Noble!" Christopher ran up to me, grabbed my bag himself, and said, "Hey—can't have someone with a bad back carrying his own bag. Oh, and since you're a return guest, I'm going to have room service send you a complimentary slice of chocolate chip cheesecake in a few minutes. Do you want your old room again, 128?"

Nine months after my last visit to his hotel, Christopher remembered multiple specific details from my previous trip. Nine months! Now, whenever I go to Palm Springs, guess where I stay? And whenever a friend or colleague says they plan to travel to Palm Springs, guess where I tell them they should stay? Do I have to tell you where? Of course, I don't.

Now again: you and I may not be as good at that as Christopher, but it's definitely a skill for us to work on. You could begin to improve this skill by writing down bullet points about your major clients to re-read before they walk in the door again. Or, you could practice saying names over and over in your head or even aloud when you first meet someone. I know some people who try to mention the other person's name at least three times within the first 30 seconds of a conversation to better engage their memory. If you know of someone who does this as well as Christopher does, ask them to share with you exactly how they do it. You may be able to glean something from them.

5. Demonstrate occasional nonverbal and verbal cues as proof of engagement. Have you ever had a conversation with someone who just stood there, motionless, with a blank expression on their face? If so, you probably stopped and asked them, "Are you still with me? Are you listening? Did I lose you?"

When you are listening to someone speak, it is particularly important to give them an occasional non-verbal cue, like nodding your head. You can even give a short verbal cue, like, "Okay…uh huh…all right…" just to reassure them that you're paying attention. Of course, you don't want to overdo the nodding, because you may end up looking like a bobblehead doll, and an "uh huh" every five seconds can be quite annoying. However, you do want to give an occasional demonstration of your full participation in the conversation. Finally:

6. Listen to understand, not simply to respond. So many people only listen to formulate a response. In fact, if you are already considering your response while the person is speaking, you have ceased to hear them. Your own inner thoughts are drowning out their spoken words. Listen to understand, not only to gather enough data to decide what you wish to say next. Be fully present in the conversation.

Great leaders are great listeners. The art of listening is so important, yet most of us have never taken a class, read an article, nor read a book on how to improve our listening skills. Since it is such an important skill, it deserves attention, practice, and skillful execution.

Now that we have discussed how to excel as a communicator, we must next talk about that all-important truth that one's circle of influence will impact one's success. Speaking and writing like a competent leader is an important skill, but certainly not the only skill a great leader will possess. Exceptional leadership doesn't occur in a vacuum; it occurs in community. Let's look at who needs to be a part of the successful leader's community.

Having The Right Support Team in Your Corner

Hang around five negative people, and you will become the sixth. Hang around five millionaires, and you will become the sixth. As a leader, it is imperative that you surround yourself with people who will encourage you to become the best version of yourself.

Clinical social worker Elizabeth Dixon writes:

> "Our relationships, more than anything else, set the stage for our health, happiness, and well-being…We are relational beings in nature, and when we're isolated or detached from a community, our health and mental health can quickly take a toll. Life is hard enough on its own. We're not meant to go about it alone."[42]

Alex Haley, internationally renowned author, was known to have kept a picture of a turtle on a fencepost on the wall of his office for many years. When asked about it, Haley responded: "Anytime you see a turtle up on top of a fence post, you know he had some help."

---

[42] Elizabeth Dixon, "The Importance of Cultivating Community: Why We Need Each Other", Psychology Today, August 20, 2021, Retrieved from https://www.psychologytoday.com/us/blog/the-flourishing-family/202108/the-importance-cultivating-community#:~:text=Key%20points,intentionality%2C%20vulnerability%2C%20and%20creativity.

No leader gets to the top of their field without a little help from some very key people. If you want to launch into the highest echelons of your leadership potential, you must surround yourself with the right supporting cast.

Below are three people I strongly recommend you have in your inner circle if you want to be successful in leadership and in life.

1. A Mentor. My definition of a mentor is someone who has already achieved what you are now trying to achieve, and who is willing to invest time in you and show you how they got there. The only people qualified to mentor you are those who have already successfully done what you are attempting to do. I would never seek relationship advice from someone who is headed to divorce court for their fourth time…I'm just sayin'.

My next book, the follow-up to this one, (which will focus more on *seasoned* leaders) will contain an entire chapter dedicated to the mentor/mentee relationship and what it should look like. For now, you already have the most important criteria for selecting a mentor: they have already achieved what you are now trying to achieve, and they are willing to invest time in you and show you how they got there. In addition, here are some other qualities you should look for in choosing a mentor:

- Your mentor is someone you respect. If you do not have respect for them - if you do not actually admire them - you will be less likely to take any advice or guidance they may offer you.
- Your mentor is someone who commits to communicating with you regularly. If they are too busy to call, Zoom, or meet with you, they are stretched too thin and would frustrate you more than inspire you. I meet with different mentees at different intervals. It all depends upon how much help and guidance they need from me.

I have one mentee with whom I have 15-minute Zoom calls once per week. Another mentee of mine whom I have known for almost ten years Zooms with me once per month, and those meetings last at least one full hour. But we also text and instant message one another several times per week. You and your mentor should come to an agreement as to your definitions of regular communication.

- Your mentor is someone who actually enjoys what they do. Remember our discussion on being jaded earlier in this book? Mentor and jaded are two words that do not belong in the same sentence. If your mentor is unhappy with their life and their career, they won't give you much positive advice, unless that advice is "Here's how not to end up like me."

But you not only need the right mentor - you need to be the right type of mentee. How can you be the type of student that a mentor will absolutely love?

1. Appreciate your mentor's time. A mentor volunteers to make themselves available to you. They do so because they care about your success, not because they're getting a salary from you. So, since your mentor is volunteering their time, it is imperative that you respect that time by a) showing up to your sessions (either virtual or in person or over the phone) on time, b) informing them well in advance if you need to reschedule, and c) thanking them for their time - each time you meet with them.

2. Demonstrate your respect for them by listening to their advice. Remember, you sought them out, not vice-versa. You approached them because of their expertise, and they demonstrated a willingness to help you. The least you can do is accept their advice and not argue or debate with them constantly. This doesn't mean you should check your

brain at the door, but it does mean that they have more experience and expertise than you do. It is disrespectful to ask someone to mentor you and then treat them as if they cannot teach you anything. If you don't respect their advice and are unwilling to listen to them, why did you ask them to mentor you in the first place?

3. Be open and honest in your communication with your mentor. Your mentor is not a mind reader, so they may not always be able to "feel" what you're needing or "feel" what you're experiencing unless you share it with them. If you need specific guidance in a specific area, clearly communicate that. A good mentor will realize that the strongest relationships are those that are more organic in nature as opposed to a mentor coming to each session with a standard, pre-designed agenda for you. Don't be afraid to tell your mentor things like, "Today, I think I really need help with…"

4. Share with your mentor your plans to immediately apply what you learn. For example, I was having a Zoom session with a mentee who told me he was feeling anxious, overwhelmed, and was having some bad dreams. While I was able to give him some guidance on how to reduce his stress and anxiety levels, I then strongly suggested that he see a licensed therapist and discuss those issues much more in depth. That same evening after our conversation, my mentee provided me with the name of the therapist he had selected, and a schedule of their future appointments. And though I told him it was not at all necessary for him to share with me anything he discussed with his therapist, he felt comfortable enough with me to do so.

While I never ask anyone to share anything that might make them uncomfortable, I do encourage every mentee to demonstrate in some way their commitment to apply the lessons learned from their mentor.

Having the right mentor in your life can provide a strong, stable foundation for your leadership. This important relationship will not only positively impact your career but will also help you to be the best you can be in every facet of your life outside of the office. However, a mentor is not the only person you need in your corner if you want to maximize your leadership potential. You will also need:

2. A Cheerleader – A cheerleader is someone whose only concern is that you never give up before you reach your goals. This person encourages you, motivates you, gives you pep talks, hugs, or high-fives, and tells you that you can do remarkable things. The cheerleader is not really concerned with your proficiency or your prowess or your performance; your cheerleader is concerned with your *perseverance*. Their main objective is to see to it that you never quit.

It's like that little old lady who approaches your child after she hears what others might consider to be your child's tone-deaf rendition of "O Holy Night" at the Christmas recital. The lady says to the child, "Oh my, that was fantastic! You are so gifted! You're going to be the next Aretha Franklin!" And don't believe for one moment that the little old lady is being dishonest. She genuinely believes that your tone-deaf child is fantastic and has enormous potential. Cheerleaders tell you that you're the greatest until you believe it and then achieve it.

3. A Butt-Kicker – This is probably the person you want the least in your life but need the most. A butt-kicker is someone who cares enough about you to look you in your eyes and tell you the uncomfortable truths about yourself that you may not *want* to hear but desperately *need* to hear. You will never grow to your full potential without someone you *invite* to keep it real with you 100 percent of the time.

The key is that this person is *invited* into your life. It should be someone who has a track record of genuine concern for you; someone who never makes you doubt that they really want the best for you. Self-appointed butt-kickers with whom you do not have a relationship of mutual respect may only engage in critique as a means of taking you down a few pegs. That attitude reeks of insecurity and jealousy on their part. The key consideration here is what is motivating them to offer their critique of you.

We all need someone who cares that we reach our greatest potential and will therefore risk hurting us in the short-term for the sake of helping us in the long-term. Your butt-kicker might tell you something like, "You know, you're being really childish about this situation. Swallow your pride, apologize to that person, and stop acting like a five-year-old."

We all need people who challenge us and push us to be our best. The right mentor, cheerleader, and butt-kicker will help you raise your effectiveness in leadership.

Mastering The Fine Art of Delegation

I'm sure you've heard it before but hearing it and knowing how to do it are not always the same thing. As a leader, you need to delegate more of your responsibilities. Giving away some of your responsibilities to the right people on your team will ensure that you have more time to deal with other important matters that you normally might not have time to adequately handle. Northwest Education, a leading business executive training organization, says the following about delegation:

"Delegation provides several advantages for both leaders and employees. It assists executives in managing their workload and increasing production, while also assisting staff in identifying and developing their strengths and working on their weaknesses...

Effective delegation also improves a team's productivity and time management by utilizing its members' existing capabilities while also allowing them to gain new information and abilities during the process…

When you delegate effectively, you can build employee trust and commitment, boost productivity, and ensure that the right people are completing the tasks that are most suited to them."[43]

There are three foundational questions the new leader should ask and answer concerning delegation. They are:

1. To whom should I delegate?
2. What is the wrong mindset concerning delegation?
3. What is the correct mindset concerning delegation?
4. What tasks should I not delegate?

Let's answer these questions so that you can master the fine art of delegation and launch your leadership into the stratosphere.

"To whom should I delegate?"

There is an art to delegation, and it begins with knowing to whom one should delegate responsibility. Fortunately, you already have the answer to this first question. As we discussed in a previous chapter, great leaders understand that they have people on their team, their Superstars, who have great attitude and great ability. Because of those qualities, the leader would be wise to delegate more responsibility to them.

Again, the *only* people on your team you should delegate more responsibility to are those people who fall into the Superstar category. They are the *only* ones who are ready for delegation. Why? Because Superstars already have stellar ability, which means you will not have to worry about the task being done well and in a timely manner. Also, the Superstar has a stellar attitude, which means they will be

---

[43] https://northwest.education/insights/careers/how-to-delegate-why-is-delegation-important/#:~:text=Delegating%20effectively%20saves%20time%2C%20helps,work%20on%20through%20your%20career.

excited about helping you share the load, and they will be honored that you consider them worthy to do so.

"What is the wrong mindset concerning delegation?"

Though most of us have heard about the importance of delegation, many leaders still fail to do it. According to Amy Gallo, contributing editor at Harvard Business Review:

> "There are plenty of reasons why managers don't delegate. Some are perfectionists who feel it's easier to do everything themselves, or that their work is better than others'...Some believe that passing on work will detract from their own importance, while others lack self-confidence and don't want to be upstaged by their subordinates."[44]

Jeffrey Pfeffer, Professor of Organizational Behavior at the Graduate School of Business, Stanford University, calls this "self-enhancement bias."[45] I often tell leaders that bragging about how the organization would fall apart without them is not a compliment. It reveals the leader's inability to lead. While it may make you feel important for an organization not to be able to function without your presence, such leaders have built their employees' dependence upon them. However, in doing so, they have failed to lead. Think about it this way: if you are a parent and your child reaches the age of 18 and can neither cook a meal for themselves nor do their own laundry, you may have loved them, but you failed to prepare them for independence.

Though your employees are not your children, your goal should be the same: to get them to stand on their own two feet and function without you having to hold their hand. In fact, that is the difference

---

[44] Amy Gallo, Why Aren't You Delegating?. Harvard Business Review. July 26, 2012. https://hbr.org/2012/07/why-arent-you-delegating

[45] Jeffrey Pfeffer, et al. Faith in Supervision and the Self-Enhancement Bias: Two Psychological Reasons Why Managers Don't Empower Workers. Basic and Applied Psychology. Volume 20, 1998. Issue 4. https://www.tandfonline.com/doi/abs/10.1207/s15324834basp2004_8

between a boss and a coach: a boss tells you what to do, but a coach equips you with what you need so that you can do it on your own. Your employees need you to coach them, not boss them. If they cannot do their job without you, you have failed them in a colossal way.

Some other indicators of the wrong mindset concerning delegation are as follows. Do any of these echo your thoughts and feelings?

- Employees should be able to keep themselves busy without my having to give them more to do.
- If I do it myself, I know it will get done the right way.
- If I give away some of my duties, my employees may perform better than I would and outshine me.
- If they execute my responsibilities too well, the company may consider me obsolete and fire me.
- By the time I explain what needs to be done, I could have already done it myself.

If any of those statements resemble your thoughts about delegation, then you have what Professor Pfeffer called self-enhancement bias and will be ineffective in your leadership role. Your goal with your staff should be to transform them all into a team of Superstars. An All-Star team of confident and competent players can outperform a team full of insecure, inexperienced rookies every time. And if the leader is insecure, what happens to the team? They either underperform or they seek out a different team or a different coach who will believe in them more than their current coach does.

"What is the correct mindset concerning delegation?"

If you are going to create shortcuts to effectiveness, which this section of the book is all about, then you must become a skillful delegator. There is no such thing as a one-person battalion in the business world. The very definition of leader means that there is someone who follows you. You are the leader of a team, and you need all members of that team functioning at their full potential to maximize team effectiveness.

Thus, delegation is an essential skill for any leader that wants their team to realize their full potential. Delegation prevents you from spreading yourself too thin, and it ensures that the Superstars on your team receive the opportunity to grow in their abilities and their creativity.

"What tasks should I absolutely not delegate?"

The answer to this question is a source of debate within the business world, but here is my take on it. I typically never delegate:

- Any task that I do not fully understand. If I delegate a task that I'm unsure how to perform, how will I be able to assist my Superstar if they come back to me and ask me for help or clarity? If I do not thoroughly understand it, I become intimately familiar with it before I delegate it.
- Any task that involves confidential information. I will never delegate a task that might involve access to an employee's personal information, such as their medical history, Social Security number, disciplinary actions of any kind, company passwords, etc. Information such as this is safer with fewer eyes involved.
- Any task your supervisor specifically informs you that they only want you to handle. If there was an assigned task that someone on my team could do better than I could, I would always speak to my supervisor about it first. In some cases, my supervisor gave me the green-light, and in other cases my supervisors stated their preference that I and I alone execute that task.

A final word should be said here about delegation. Trust your Superstar: they wouldn't be Superstars if they needed you to micromanage them. Once you delegate a task to a Superstar, get out of their way and let them handle it. Let them know that you will be available to consult with them if they have a question or if they get stuck but reassure them "You're a Superstar; you've got this."

Also, it's perfectly okay for you to keep some tasks on your plate that you could delegate, but you just happen to really enjoy. Work should be enjoyable, so if there is something you particularly like to do, that's fine. For example, you really do enjoy leading staff meetings, but there is a member of your team who could do it equally as well. You could continue to lead staff meetings, but also be willing to allow that team member to "guest host" every now and then. Just be sure that not all your tasks fall into the "I love this too much to give it up" category.

Wrap-up

Let's review what you have learned in this chapter:

- Most employees consider their supervisors to be poor communicators.
- How communication skills affect every leadership task, without exception.
- Effective communication is a skill that can be improved upon.
- Why the right words and tone are such essential components of effective communication.
- The importance of nonverbal communication, such as body positioning, facial expressions, and physical appearance, and how to improve each of them.
- Written communication should focus on being understood rather than on being impressive.

- Several practical tips for ensuring your written communication is clearer and better understood.
- Six tips to help you become a better listener.
- How to choose the right support team to help you on your leadership journey.
- Why you should delegate, to whom you should delegate, and tasks you should not delegate.

Let's look at our action steps based upon the information in this chapter.

Chapter 4 Implementation Tasks:

1. Sign yourself up for some one-on-one coaching with a speech coach/communications coach. Enroll in a training seminar on public speaking skills or on business writing skills. Start regularly reading articles or books on speaking skills.
2. Use any or all the six listed methods for getting to know your employees' strengths and weaknesses.
3. Go back through some of your work emails from the past month or so and look for any sentences longer than 12 words or so. Rewrite each one so that it has a maximum of five words. You will be surprised at how easily you can get the same point across with fewer words.
4. Practice the six listening skills and ask someone to hold you accountable for putting them into practice quickly and often.
5. Decide who will be your mentor, your cheerleader, and your butt-kicker. Then, specifically ask them to fulfill those roles for you. Try NOT to have one person fill all three roles. Why? Because if - God forbid - something was to happen to that one person and you could no longer communicate

with them, you would be completely without *any* of the three essential people in your corner.

6. Decide which of your job duties you can delegate, and then give them to your Superstars. Remember: The Superstars are the *only* ones to whom you should delegate responsibility.

Chapter 4 Reactions:

1. What did I already know?

2. Of what was I reminded? How will I act upon those reminders?

3. What was brand new information to me?

During my campaign speech for Student Body President in my senior year at Little Rock Central High School, I told a story about a balloon salesperson. That story has meant so much to me over the years, and I present it now as my closing thought for this book.

There once was a man who sold balloons in the park. He sold every color one could imagine: orange, red, yellow, green...every bright, pretty color in the rainbow. Whenever his sales were a little low, he would release one of the balloons into the air, and people all over the park would see the beautiful balloon and rush over to the salesman to buy one. By using this tactic, the salesman never really had any "bad days." One day, he was approached by a little boy who said, "Mister, I love those pretty colored balloons, but what would happen if you were to release a black balloon into the air? Black isn't as pretty as red, is it? Black isn't as pretty as blue, is it? If you released a black balloon, would anybody want one?" The salesman smiled at the little boy, and released yet another balloon into the air, and both he and the boy watched it as it flew high above the crowd. The salesman then said, "Son, it's not the color of the balloon that matters; it's what INSIDE that makes it rise!"

New leader, you have greatness inside of you. You have that magical quality that will allow you to rise to the top in every area of life. My hope is that this book has given you even more of the necessary tools to launch you into your leadership legacy. Take what you have learned and go make a permanent, positive impact upon this world. I believe in you.

BIBLIOGRAPHY

Ashford, Kate. *How To manage Toxic Employees.* Monster.com. https://www.monster.com/career- advice/article/manage-a-toxic-employee

Calvert, Deb Calvert. *10 Signs You Are (or could be) an Emerging Leader.* LinkedIn. March 24, 2015 https://www.linkedin.com/pulse/10-signs-you-could-emerging-leader-deb-calvert/

Carver, Sarah. *Great Leaders Prioritize. Sigma Assessment Systems.* https://www.sigmaassessmentsystems.com/prioritize/#:~:text-t=Prioritizing%20involves%20identifying%20 critical%20 tasks,scramble%20as%20key%20deadlines%20approach.

Covey, Stephen. 2020. *The 7 Habits of Highly Effective People, 30th Anniv. Ed.* New York: Simon and Schuster.

Dixon, Elizabeth. *The Importance of Cultivating Community: Why We Need Each Other.* Psychology Today, August 20, 2021, Retrieved from https://www.psychologytoday.com/us/blog/the-flourishing-family/202108/the- importance-cultivating community#:~:text=Key%20points,intentionality%2C%20 vulnerability%2C%20and%20creativity.

Fripp, Patricia. *Preparing and Presenting Powerful Talks.* (audio lecture, Toastmasters International, circa 2000).

Gallo, Amy Gallo. *Why Aren't You Delegating?* Harvard Business Review. July 26, 2012. https://hbr.org/2012/07/why-arent-you-delegating

Gambill, Tony. *Leadership Practices to Prioritize Your Time and Energy.* Forbes.com. August 25, 2021. https://www.forbes.com/sites/tonygambill/2021/08/25/3-leadership-practices-to-prioritize-your-time-and- energy/?sh=2d3201d714ff

https://dictionary.apa.org/stress

https://familiesforlife.sg/discover-an-article/pages/30-ways-to-spend-more-family-time.aspx

https://northwest.education/insights/careers/how-to-delegate-why-is-delegation- important/#:~:text=Delegating%20 effectively%20saves%20time%2C%20helps,work%20 on%20through% 20your%20career.

https://online.hbs.edu/blog/post/leadership- communication#:~:text= A%20leader%20is%20someone%20who,goals%2C%20 and%20inspire%20positiv e%20change.

https://www.brainyquote.com/authors/napoleon-hill-quotes

https://www.brainyquote.com/authors/steve-jobs-quotes

https://www.coloniallife.com/about/newsroom/2019/march/ stressed-workers-costing-employers-billions

https://www.health.harvard.edu/staying-healthy/exercising-to-relax

https://www.linerun.co/what-is-an-emerging-leader

https://www.masterclass.com/articles/smart-casual-dress-code-and-attire-guide

https://www.mayoclinic.org/healthy-lifestyle/stress-management/in-depth/exercise-and-stress/art- 20044469#:~:text=Examples%20include%20walking%2C%20stair%20climbing,Pencil%20it%20in.

https://www.myshortlister.com/insights/workplace-stress-statistics

https://www.psychologytoday.com/us/basics/self-talk

https://www.quotespedia.org/authors/k/kimberly-jones/dont-let-people-pull-you-into-their-storm-pull-them-into- your-peace-kimberly-jones/

https://www.wisefamousquotes.com/shania-twain-quotes/a-friend-is-someone-who-knows-the-song-2196580/

Lucas, Stephen E. 2012. *The Art of Public Speaking.* New York: McGrawiHill. 11th ed.

Maidenberg, Michelle P. 6 Tips for Making Difficult Decisions." *Psychology Today,* March 16, 2021, Retrieved from: https://libguides.heidelberg.edu/chicago/article#:~:text=Footnote%2FEndnote&text=Last%20Name%2C%20%22Article%20Title%2C,necessary)%2C%22%20page%20cited.

Maizur, Caitlin. *40+ Worrisome Workplace Stress Statistics [2022]: Facts, Causes, and Trends.* Zippia. January 23, 2022. https://www.zippia.com/advice/workplace-stress-statistics/

Odeven, Ed Odeven. *Words of wisdom: Coaching advice from Lenny Wilkens,* TalkBasket.net. September 8, 2019. https://www.talkbasket.net/44486-words-of-wisdom-coaching-advice-from-lenny-wilkens

Pfeffer, Jeffrey et al. *Faith in Supervision and the Self-Enhancement Bias: Two Psychological Reasons Why Managers Don't Empower Workers.* Basic and Applied Psychology. Volume 20, 1998. Issue 4. https://www.tandfonline.com/doi/abs/10.1207/s15324834basp2004_8

Rea, Kathleen. *"I'm sorry my actions triggered you": Apoloigies that deflect responsibility.* October 30, 2021. https://contactimprov-consentculture.com/2021/10/30/im-sorry-my-actions-trig-gered-you-apologies-that- deflect-responsibility-and-can-set-the-stage-for-abusive-behaviors/

Schmidt, Emily. *Reading the numbers: 130 million american adults have low literacy skills, but funding differs drastically by state.* American Public Media. March 16, 2022. https://www.apmre-searchlab.org/10x-adult- literacy

Schuller, Robert H. 1984. *Tough Times Never Last, But Tough People Do!* New York: Bantam Books.

Schwantes, Marcel. *Survey: 91 Percent of 1,000 Employees Say Their Bosses Lack This 1 Critical Skill.* Inc.com. https://www.inc.com/marcel-schwantes/survey-91-percent-of-1000-employees-say-their-boss.html

Starner, Tom Starner. *Survey: Boss'bad communication skills drag the company down.* HR Dive. June 25, 2015. https://www.hrdive.com/news/survey-bosss-bad-communication-skills-drag-the-company-down/401263/

Stith-Flood, Charlotte. *It's Not Hard to Be Humble: The Role of Humility in Leadership.* American Academy of Family Physicians. June 2018. https://www.aafp.org/pubs/fpm/issues/2018/0500/p25.html#:~:text=Humility%20is%20an%20important%20but,as%20a%20leader's%20responsibility%20increases.

Surrett, Ethan. *How Workplace Attire Affects Employee Perceptions and Organizational Culture."* Honors thesis, University of Southern Mississippi, 2021, iv, https://aquila.usm.edu/cgi/viewcontent.cgi?article=1784&context=honors_theses

Williams, Scott Williams. *Listening Effectively.* Wright State University. http://www.wright.edu/~scott.williams/LeaderLetter/listening.htm#:~:text=Research%20has%20found%20 that%20 by,in%20the%20people%20you%20manage.

Wood, John. *15 Tips for Reducing Your Learning Curve.* American Writers and Artists Institute. April 18, 2012.